P9-COP-615

DATE DUE

823
Rea   Readings on Cry, the
         beloved country

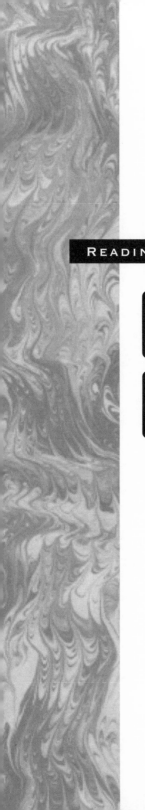

READINGS ON

CRY, THE BELOVED COUNTRY

OTHER TITLES IN THE GREENHAVEN PRESS LITERARY COMPANION SERIES:

WORLD AUTHORS

Fyodor Dostoyevsky
Homer
Sophocles

WORLD LITERATURE

All Quiet on the Western
  Front
Antigone
Candide
Crime and Punishment
Cyrano de Bergerac
The Diary of a Young Girl
A Doll's House
Medea
Night
One Day in the Life of
  Ivan Denisovich
The Stranger

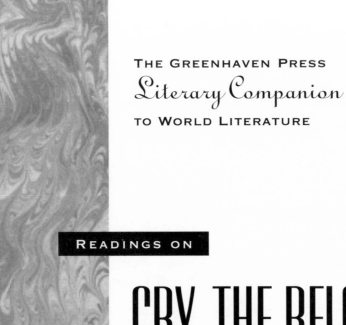

THE GREENHAVEN PRESS
Literary Companion
TO WORLD LITERATURE

READINGS ON

CRY, THE BELOVED COUNTRY

Estella Baker Gerstung, *Book Editor*

David L. Bender, *Publisher*
Bruno Leone, *Executive Editor*
Bonnie Szumski, *Series Editor*

Greenhaven Press, Inc., San Diego, CA

Every effort has been made to trace the owners of copy-righted material. The articles in this volume may have been edited for content, length, and/or reading level. The titles have been changed to enhance the editorial purpose. Those interested in locating the original source will find the complete citation on the first page of each article.

Library of Congress Cataloging-in-Publication Data

Readings on Cry, the beloved country / Estella Gerstung, book editor.
    p. cm. — (The Greenhaven Press literary companion to world literature)
    Includes bibliographical references and index.
    ISBN 0-7377-0431-4 (pbk. : alk. paper) —
ISBN 0-7377-0432-2 (lib. bdg. : alk. paper)
    1. Paton, Alan. Cry, the beloved country. 2. South Africa—In literature. 3. Race relations in literature. 4. Apartheid in literature. I. Title: Cry, the beloved country. II. Paton, Alan. III. Gerstung, Estella. IV. Series.

PR9369.3.P37 C737 2001
923'.914—dc21

                               00-064693
                                  CIP

Cover photo: Archive Photos

Copyright © 2001 by Greenhaven Press, Inc.
PO Box 289009
San Diego, CA 92198-9009
Printed in the U.S.A.

"At the end the greatest achievement for me was not its success or its critical acclaim but the fascination I discovered in the children as they read it and talked to me about it."

—Alan Paton, April 1988
about *Cry, the Beloved Country*

CONTENTS

and tragedy without neglecting the capacity of human beings to love and forgive one another.

Chapter 3: Politics and
Cry, the Beloved Country

Monye dismisses *Cry, the Beloved Country*'s thesis, "Love thy neighbor as thyself," as an inadequate sermon, and declares, "It is doubtful how love would work when fear rules the lives of both races in South Africa."

FOREWORD

"'Tis the good reader that
makes the good book."

Ralph Waldo Emerson

The story's bare facts are simple: The captain, an old and scarred seafarer, walks with a peg leg made of whale ivory. He relentlessly drives his crew to hunt the world's oceans for the great white whale that crippled him. After a long search, the ship encounters the whale and a fierce battle ensues. Finally the captain drives his harpoon into the whale, but the harpoon line catches the captain about the neck and drags him to his death.

A simple story, a straightforward plot—yet, since the 1851 publication of Herman Melville's *Moby-Dick*, readers and critics have found many meanings in the struggle between Captain Ahab and the whale. To some, the novel is a cautionary tale that depicts how Ahab's obsession with revenge leads to his insanity and death. Others believe that the whale represents the unknowable secrets of the universe and that Ahab is a tragic hero who dares to challenge fate by attempting to discover this knowledge. Perhaps Melville intended Ahab as a criticism of Americans' tendency to become involved in well-intentioned but irrational causes. Or did Melville model Ahab after himself, letting his fictional character express his anger at what he perceived as a cruel and distant god?

Although literary critics disagree over the meaning of *Moby-Dick*, readers do not need to choose one particular interpretation in order to gain an understanding of Melville's

9

novel. Instead, by examining various analyses, they can gain numerous insights into the issues that lie under the surface of the basic plot. Studying the writings of literary critics can also aid readers in making their own assessments of *Moby-Dick* and other literary works and in developing analytical thinking skills.

The Greenhaven Literary Companion Series was created with these goals in mind. Designed for young adults, this unique anthology series provides an engaging and comprehensive introduction to literary analysis and criticism. The essays included in the Literary Companion Series are chosen for their accessibility to a young adult audience and are expertly edited in consideration of both the reading and comprehension levels of this audience. In addition, each essay is introduced by a concise summation that presents the contributing writer's main themes and insights. Every anthology in the Literary Companion Series contains a varied selection of critical essays that cover a wide time span and express diverse views. Wherever possible, primary sources are represented through excerpts from authors' notebooks, letters, and journals and through contemporary criticism.

Each title in the Literary Companion Series pays careful consideration to the historical context of the particular author or literary work. In-depth biographies and detailed chronologies reveal important aspects of authors' lives and emphasize the historical events and social milieu that influenced their writings. To facilitate further research, every anthology includes primary and secondary source bibliographies of articles and/or books selected for their suitability for young adults. These engaging features make the Greenhaven Literary Companion series ideal for introducing students to literary analysis in the classroom or as a library resource for young adults researching the world's great authors and literature.

Exceptional in its focus on young adults, the Greenhaven Literary Companion Series strives to present literary criticism in a compelling and accessible format. Every title in the series is intended to spark readers' interest in leading American and world authors, to help them broaden their understanding of literature, and to encourage them to formulate their own analyses of the literary works that they read. It is the editors' hope that young adult readers will find these anthologies to be true companions in their study of literature.

INTRODUCTION

Cry, the Beloved Country is a novel of universal human emotions: fear and joy, anger and love, selfishness and generosity, deceit and friendship, suffering and compassion. It is the journey of one man's and yet of every human's life.

In part, the importance of *Cry, the Beloved Country* lies in its celebration of what is positive in the human spirit. Three characters in this novel—Stephen Kumalo, Arthur Jarvis, and Theophilus Msimangu—show deep concern for their fellow humans, and each one acts out of compassion and love for others. Each looks to the future and works to make it better than the present. Each inspires others even when not expecting to.

Cry, the Beloved Country works as history as well. Apartheid and its devastating effects on all the people of South Africa are accurately portrayed by Paton. Grinding poverty, blatant discrimination, and the determination of some South Africans to overcome these national blights were all a part of Alan Paton's world, and he captured that reality in his novel.

Like other classics, however, *Cry, the Beloved Country* shows certain lasting truths and values quite apart from history. It shows humans as imperfect but capable of the noble, as limited but rich in possibility and hope. It shows despair as something to be forever resisted. It shows that while hate contracts a person's power, love expands it. What gives *Cry, the Beloved Country* universality is this true picture of the range of human nature, from degradation to transcendence.

A reader will recognize that one of the major themes of *Cry, the Beloved Country* is racial prejudice and fear. The novel shows that fear can prove divisive and destructive, but that those who retain the capacity to love can ease racial tensions and suffering, and work for a better life for all citizens. *Cry, the Beloved Country* portrays the evils in society balanced by the goodness of individuals. Thus, there is comfort from good people even in the midst of the desolation.

Reading this novel will challenge a student to solve problems, both personal and on a larger scale, and lead to an increased understanding of others. The readings in this volume are chosen to aid the student in appreciating *Cry, the Beloved Country.* The authors of the individual viewpoints focus on the major themes of the novel, on the novel's impact on South Africa, and on the way the novel affected individual readers. In addition, a brief biography of Alan Paton provides insights into his motives for writing the novel and into the sources of many of the characters and settings in the book.

The readings in this volume come with helpful features for those new to literary criticism. Each essay's introduction summarizes the article's main ideas. In addition, each introduction provides background on the author of the essay and gives a bit of background on the author. Notes explain difficult or unfamiliar words and concepts throughout the book. Together with the essays themselves, these features aim to enhance the reader's appreciation and understanding of *Cry, the Beloved Country.*

ALAN PATON: A BIOGRAPHY

A stern father and a mother who taught Alan Paton to read and write, along with an intense love of nature and a deeply religious, simple lifestyle were all part of his preschool years. He loved birds, the sight of green rolling hills, of brightly colored flowers, of a firefly, of water flowing over stones in a river, and the rare sight of a shy, small antelope.

SOUTH AFRICAN FAMILY

Born January 11, 1903, Alan Paton was the first child of James Paton, an immigrant to South Africa from Scotland, and Eunice, who had been born in South Africa. They lived in Pietermaritzburg, a city with a population of 30,000 that was the capital of the South African province of Natal. Other older relatives who figured in Alan's childhood were his paternal grandmother, who lived with his family, and an aunt who had migrated with her brother and had become a teacher. Never marrying, she lavished affection on Alan, his younger brother Atholl, and his two sisters, Eunice and Ailsa. His mother, aunt, and grandmother set an example for Alan of self-control and love, for he did not remember a single cross word between his mother and either his grandmother or his aunt.

Alan's father was an intelligent man, who despite having left school at the age of fourteen, was a minor poet who also served as a stenographer in the Supreme Court in Pietermaritzburg. James Paton was deferential to those he worked for, but he was strict to the point of cruelty at home, at least with his three older children. The one exception was the youngest child, Ailsa, to whom he showed greater kindness.

PRECOCIOUS PUPIL

Alan excelled in school, even skipping several grades. On the playground he was a shy, small boy eager for recess or lunch to be over. Accustomed to doing as he was told, Alan was well-liked by his teachers. Because he was smaller than his older classmates, he was also the target of bullies, and the result was trouble for Alan. One afternoon, when some bigger boys told him to push a girl off the sidewalk, he did so, partly because he was used to obeying and partly from fear of them. The principal, knowing how to fit the punishment to the offense, made him eat lunch with the girls. It was several years before he was comfortable at school outside the classroom.

When he was eleven, two important events occurred. First, his family moved to a larger home that seemed like a mansion to Alan. Now he and Atholl had a small room of their own instead of sleeping on the verandah. The second major event was his entering Pietermaritzburg's Maritzburg College, roughly equivalent to an American high school except that his school was only for middle and upper-middle-class white boys.

Although Alan remained an assiduous reader, he began to pay less attention to his studies than before, and more attention to joining his classmates in witticisms and clowning around. He had regularly been first in his class; now he slipped to second or third and did not recall his parents saying anything about it.

The strictness with which James Paton treated his sons, however, did not ease as they grew. Every Saturday Alan's father made him and Atholl work in the garden. They resented this as their friends went by, waving and joking, on their way to playing sports. Alan nevertheless developed from this chore a lifelong love of gardening and eventually had an extensive flower garden that he and hired help worked in.

While at Maritzburg College, Alan thought of becoming a doctor, but his father explained that this would not be financially possible because medical school was too expensive for the family to afford. There was no help available in the form of loans. Alan therefore accepted the suggestion he train to be a teacher, as the government was offering scholarships that paid for fees and books to would-be teachers. In addition, the government offered education students a stipend of £80 a year. Alan had been strong in liberal arts, but since science teachers were needed, when he went to Natal University College, he concentrated on math and physics.

Alan's parents by this time expected their son to contribute to the family's finances. Of the £80, therefore, he paid his parents £60 for board and room, and from the remainder paid for his books, clothes, bus rides, and all other expenses.

Alan's parents readily approved of the friend whom Alan chose as his model, Railton Dent, son of a missionary, highly principled and popular with adults and peers alike. Six years Alan's senior, but a freshman like him at Natal University College, Dent had already served as a non-graduate school principal, but determined to graduate and make the education of black Africans his life's work. From Dent, Paton took his guiding principle—that life was not worth living unless lived for a purpose greater than oneself.

Always an avid and wide-ranging reader of American, English, and South African literature, at the university Alan continued that pastime. He and Neville Nuttell, a younger friend he made at the university, used to sit on a bench in a cemetery near the campus and discuss the great works of English authors such as Shakespeare, Milton, Wordsworth, Coleridge, Byron, Shelley, Keats, Tennyson, and Browning.

Paton exemplified the belief that for a good life one develops body, mind, and soul. In addition to his steady reading and scientific studies, he attended church regularly. His was a life of faith. It was a journey towards a symbolic destination which the prophet Isaiah described as a "holy mountain," a place where people and animals "shall not hurt or destroy," attainable only after death.

Paton paid attention not only to his studies and his faith, but also to his physical well-being. To develop his body, he participated in several sports. With Railton Dent, he ran three or four miles two or three evenings a week. He played rugby, cricket, and tennis. With friends, especially Reginald Pearse, Paton learned to take marathon walks, the two of them walking on one occasion fifty-two miles in a single day.

FIRST TRIP OVERSEAS

Although he had been shy as a child, at Natal University Paton flourished. He wrote articles for the students' magazine, and took part in formal debates. His skill as a debater, coupled with his talent for holding the attention of an audience, made him a natural student politician. When he was eighteen, the 223 students at Natal University elected Paton president of the Students' Representative Council. While he was president again the next year, fellow students raised funds to send him to London to represent them at a student conference.

The trip to England was a grand experience. He stayed with an upper middle class family with maids and a butler.

Feeling like a country bumpkin, he knocked over a china tea set. Luckily, his gracious hosts would not let him pay for a new set. Because of this refusal, Alan still had enough money to buy a motorcycle and, with a friend he made at the conference, cycle through England and Scotland. This trip introduced him to people beyond the confines of his hometown and South Africa, to countries he had hitherto only heard and read about.

TEACHING AND LOVE

When it was time for his final university examinations, Alan felt confident in math, but not in physics. Ironically, when the results came out, he had passed physics but failed math. He did some part-time teaching while he studied another year, and that time he passed math with good marks.

With his university degree in hand, in 1925 Paton began teaching at Ixopo High School, a co-educational institution some 55 miles from his hometown. While there, he met his future wife. He loved his Ixopo students, and soon after going there also fell in love with a young woman, Doris (Dorrie) Francis Lusted, six years older than he and married. He met her on the tennis courts; they played tennis often. Paton was unable to hide his feelings. One evening he was one of several guests at the Lusted home, and after the guests left, Dorrie's husband told her, "That young man is in love with you."

Dorrie's husband had been in ill health for some time, and within three months after Paton and Dorrie met, Lusted died of tuberculosis. Dorrie moved back to her parents' home and donned the traditional black clothes of mourning. After a mourning period of several months, Dorrie resumed seeing Paton. They met again on the tennis courts and she began inviting him to dinner at Morningside, her parents' home. It was not long before Paton had confessed his love to Dorrie, and she had told him that she felt likewise. As he went home that night, Alan felt as if the gates of heaven had opened to him.

In September 1928 Alan Paton and Dorrie married in Ixopo in the Anglican church. Although Paton had been raised a Christadelphian, he was attracted to the rituals of Anglican worship. Eventually, he joined the Anglican church, in part because he and Dorrie (who was already Anglican) planned to have children, and Paton believed that children should be raised in a church that both parents attended.

CAREER CHANGE

Another event that changed Paton's life was his contracting typhoid fever, also called enteric fever, at the age of thirty-two. Paton was dangerously ill. His weight dropped from 150 pounds to 90 before he rallied. During the months of recovery, Paton had time to reflect on where his life was heading, and as a result, he decided he did not want to go on teaching the sons of the wealthy.

From his reading of *The Young Delinquent* by Cyril Burt as well as books by Sheldon, Eleanor Glueck, and Homer Lane, he had become interested in youthful offenders. Now, he turned to Jans Hofmyer, a friend he had made in 1927 when he was helping, as Hofmyer was, at a summer camp for boys, sponsored by the Students' Christian Association. They worked together there for several summers. In 1934 with the help of Hofmyer, Deputy Prime Minister of South Africa, Paton applied for a position as warden—of a white reformatory, or of a colored reformatory, or of the largest reformatory in South Africa, Diepkloof, the predominantly black one just outside Johannesburg. He received an appointment to the black reformatory, and had to take a pay cut to accept it.

In 1934 the South African parliament had transferred all its reformatories from the Department of Prisons to the Union Education Department. The Education Department naturally decided to appoint people from the world of education to head the reformatories. Liberal leaders, Prime Minister Jan Christian Smuts and his Deputy Minister of Education, Jans Hendrik Hofmyer, promoted the change, but Hofmyer told Paton it was hard to see what could be done at Diepkloof. Still, Paton welcomed the challenge.

Boys could be sent to Diepkloof for offenses as minor as stealing a piece of fruit or as violent as murder. They entered a reformatory that looked forbidding. It began with a high outer gate and 13-foot fence topped with barbed wire that surrounded the whole reformatory. There was also an inner gate with offices on either side of it, opening to the parade ground, dormitory rooms, hospital, solitary confinement cells, and kitchen. When Paton arrived, the gate guards and the boys inside the yard lined up in military style for parade, saluted, and greeted him.

REFORMATORY CHANGES

On Paton's first morning at Diepkloof he went for what was called the opening of the cells and discovered their unspeakable stench. Paton found that for 14 hours of every 24, 20 boys in each of 20 rooms were locked in with only one bucket of water to drink and one in which to urinate and defecate.

Paton set about to put his personal stamp on Diepkloof. He enjoyed the freedom he was given in leading the institution, although he found that at first the staff resisted the changes he wanted to make. Paton worked to improve sanitation by having latrines dug and by getting permission for the boys to have unlimited access to them. He gradually had all dormitory cells opened all 24 hours of the day. These, however, were only two of the important changes Paton worked for.

Paton was grateful for changes in the reformatory's image that were decreed by a Department of Education administrator: The boys were now to be called pupils, and the warden and his deputy were to be called Principal and Vice-Principal. Even the way the boys at Diepkloof were to describe their surroundings changed. In Afrikaans, *die tronk*, the prison, became *die skool*, the school.

Paton introduced more changes to allow the boys some opportunity for creative self-expression. When he succeeded in getting the walls inside the dormitory whitewashed, he let the boys both draw and paint on them.

Paton had for some time believed that a reformatory's mission was not so much to punish as to teach its inmates how to handle freedom once it had been regained. To do that, he believed he needed to grant the boys some freedom before they were released. When Paton would have his staff introduce a new measure of freedom, a spontaneous cheer would go up from the boys. When the bell sounded calling for silence, compliance was immediate. Paton felt that such respect shown when a privilege was granted was the beginning of the reform he hoped would be successful. Paton's hopes were fulfilled when within his first year, on January 1, 1936 the big front gates and front portion of the fence were taken down.

THE VAKASHA

Other reforms followed. As part of his reforms, Paton was able to institute a code of honor whereby boys who had been at Diepkloof at least nine months and had shown responsibility could have Sunday afternoons free to roam the large farm that was part of the institution so long as they returned by five o'clock. Before receiving permission for these outings, however, the boys took part in a ceremony Paton devised. Called up one by one on the parade ground, after Paton pinned a red cloth to the boy's shirt pocket, the pupil turned, faced the assembled boys, and made a pledge:

> Today I receive my vakasha badge. [In Zulu, vakasha means "to go for a walk."]
> I promise not to go beyond the boundaries of the farm.
> I promise not to touch anything that is not mine.
> I promise to obey the rules of the school.

The system proved effective. Students took the pledge seriously. Absconding dropped from 13 per month in 1935 when the boys could not easily escape to 3 per month in 1948 when more than half the boys, granted increased freedom, could easily escape. When two boys turned themselves in after absconding, one having gone 450 miles to Durban, each boy told police he had returned because of "the promise."

Paton continued to institute ways to ease the transition of the boys from life at Diepkloof to freedom outside it. In an effort to provide them with usable skills, he introduced trades such as shoemaking and tailoring. Those who proved themselves responsible with Sunday afternoon freedom were eventually granted home leaves.

To move the boys out of the big dormitory rooms into something more like what they would be living in after leaving the reformatory, Paton succeeded in having a major addition to the reformatory built on an open piece of land below the main block. This new complex with its central playground housed in each of four cottages 25 boys as well as an African teacher and his wife who served as housemother, and in each of 25 huts five boys, thus accommodating all together 200 of the most responsible pupils.

Despite such major reforms, Paton regretted that the number of boys earning privileges was not higher. Word of the reforms, nevertheless, spread outside Diepkloof, and the number of its students increased steadily between 1935 and 1948—from 400 to 700.

THE BISHOP'S COMMISSION

While principal at Diepkloof, Paton did not neglect his religion. He and Ben Moloi, head teacher and Anglican, re-

quested from the Bishop of Johannesburg a monthly communion service at the reformatory. Attendance was voluntary as
it was for the confirmation class Paton and Moloi trained. All
thirteen years, moreover, while Paton was reformatory principal, he also served as a representative to the annual synod,
the governing council of the churches in the area.

Paton's spiritual devotion was something Bishop Clayton
took note of. When in 1941 Clayton formed a commission to
"define what it believed to be the mind of Christ for South
Africa," Paton was one of thirty-three members. For two
years, the Commission met one evening every week. Clayton
himself wrote the Commission's final report that covered the
following conclusions: To change society and the individual
to believe the truth that all men were brothers would require
a change of will. It was hypocritical for white South Africa
and its government to say they were fighting for the rights of
men so long as they were refusing to grant rights to any of
its people because of color. The Commission further condemned the gross inequality in income, the system of mi-
gratory labor, and the shocking state of housing for blacks.
It condemned occupational segregation—reserving certain
kinds of labor for specific racial groups, and the inequality
of funds and equipment for educating them. Dealing with its
most difficult consideration, the vote, the Commission concluded that the franchise should be extended to Colored, In-
dian, and African men. With a common voting roll for citizens, members of parliament would represent all qualified
voters. To effect these changes, the Commission decided
there would have to be "a change of heart within the nation"
and that the nation should be "called back to God."

Not all members of the Commission considered its find-
ings realistic, especially the change-of-heart and return-to-
God clause. Chief among the dissenters was Alfred Hoernlé,
Professor of Philosophy at Witwatersrand and President of
the South African Institute of Race Relations. Clayton, after
listening to the opposition until he could bear it no more,
jumped to his feet and thundered:

> The Church is not here primarily to serve society. Its prime
> duty is to worship God and obey Him. And if it is God's will
> that we should serve society in this way or that, then it is our
> duty to do it. Let us therefore be very careful that it is God's
> will we are trying to obey, and that we are not merely trying
> to make the Church do something that we want to be done.

That quelled the opposition. As for Paton, he said that the Commission's work did not change South Africa, but that it changed him. He was beginning to see the oppressed situation of the blacks and to see them as equals who should have the vote, thus sharing in the rule of the country.

OVERSEAS TOUR OF REFORMATORIES AND PRISONS

A few years after the work of the Commission, emboldened by his success at Diepkloof, Paton prepared to apply for the post of director of all the reformatories and prisons in South Africa. To do so he obtained a six-month leave of absence so he could tour similar facilities in Russia, England, Canada, and the United States. Unable to obtain a visa for Russia, he substituted Sweden for that part of his itinerary.

Financing such a trip would not be easy for Paton, but he put together several ways to do so. His department gave him paid leave for three months. He sold his own insurance policies. Dorrie agreed to help earn money by going to work as a secretary. Knowing that the Society of Christians and Jews was holding a conference in London just before he would start his tour, he appealed to that organization for funds. In September 1940, shortly before South Africa entered the second World War, Paton had joined the Society of Christians and Jews to help combat anti-Semitism, which in the 1930s had grown not only in Europe but was spreading in his own country among extreme Nationalists. The Society agreed to pay Paton's plane fare to London on condition he attend the conference and report back to the Society. This he gladly did.

Following the conference in London, Paton began a rigorous schedule of reformatory and prison visits, first in England and Sweden. As he had planned all along, he took a side trip to Norway, home of the Nobel Prize–winning author Knut Hamsun whose novel, *Growth of the Soil*, he had read and enjoyed as a student.

HOMESICKNESS AND HIS NOVEL

One evening in Norway, while waiting to meet a friend for dinner, Paton, homesick, sat down at his hotel room's desk and wrote about a road he and Dorrie had often walked years earlier: "There is a lovely road that runs from Ixopo into the hills." He kept writing with no conscious intention. But before his friend came to take him to dinner, he had finished the first short chapter of *Cry, the Beloved Country.*

Once he had started, Paton wrote wherever he could, mostly in hotel rooms after a day's activities. To regain the drive he needed to continue, he had only to read what he had already written, and the strong emotion would return.

CHARACTERS AND PLOT BASED ON REAL PEOPLE

The novel was a product of Paton's own experience, and he drew on people he knew as he created his characters. Reverend Stephen Kumalo, for instance, was modeled after an elderly blind priest who brought food and gifts to his son, who was confined to Diepkloof. The old man's love for his son was not at all lessened by the fact that the young man had been jailed for stealing. The plot was also inspired by real events. The murder of Arthur Jarvis, for example, was based on a murder committed by one of Diepkloof's students while he was on a Sunday afternoon leave.

Paton finished the novel on Christmas Eve, exactly three months after he began it. At that time he was in San Francisco visiting friends he had met earlier in his travels. At a Christmas Eve party, he shared a small table with two other guests, Aubrey and Marigold Burns, who invited him to their home for Christmas Day. Paton mentioned he had written a novel, and offered to let them read it. Both Burnses were deeply moved by what they read, and Aubrey told Paton, "This book will go on living long after you are dead."

FINDING A PUBLISHER

The Burnses wanted to help Paton find a publisher before he left the United States. They arranged for friends to type day and night, making fifteen copies of the first six chapters, and sent them to publishers with the request that if interested, the publisher write to Alan Paton at one of his destinations, in Ontario, Canada.

When he reached Ontario, Paton found that he already had letters from nine interested publishers. Scribners, a company he greatly respected, had expressed interest, so he asked the Burnses to type up the remaining chapters and send them to Scribners. Upon his arrival in New York early in January, Paton went at once to Scribners' offices. Not only did Scribners accept the book, but they published it without making a single change. In return for the Burnses' help, Paton named Aubrey and Marigold as his agents, which entitled them to 10 percent of the royalties the novel earned.

Paton's tour of prisons and reformatories was at an end. On his four week boat journey home, he wrote a fifty-page report on what he had learned. Among other things, he had found that Diepkloof Reformatory compared favorably with any of the prisons and reformatories he had toured in Sweden, England, the United States, and Canada. Back home, he resumed work at Diepkloof and talked to no one but Dorrie about his novel.

RAVE REVIEWS

The first reviews of *Cry, the Beloved Country*, published February 1, 1948, guaranteed success for the novel. A review by Orville Prescott in *The New York Times* said, "A beautiful and profoundly moving story, a story steeped in sadness and grief but radiant with hope and compassion." Margaret Carson Hubbard of *The Herald Tribune* wrote, "As a novel, a story of lives unfolding, *Cry, the Beloved Country* stands by any standards. But above all, the quality of the style is a new experience." The first printing sold out the first day and by April the novel was in its sixth printing.

Charles Scribner himself wrote what at the time were to Paton the most meaningful words: "You should be here—it is most exciting but exhausting. In my thirty-five years of publishing, I have never known the like." Scribner predicted the novel would sell hundreds of thousands of copies.

THE MUSICAL AND FILMS

The impact of *Cry, the Beloved Country* soon was felt beyond the literary world. March 2, 1948 Scribner cabled Paton in South Africa, to tell him that film director Sir Alexander Korda of London Films wanted to buy the film rights. Soon thereafter Scribner cabled again to say that Pulitzer Prize–winning American playwright Maxwell Anderson wanted to buy the world dramatic rights.

London's *Sunday Times* awarded Paton its annual £1,000 book prize for *Cry, the Beloved Country*, a prize he shared with Winston Churchill for *The Gathering Storm* and with Frederick Sheldon for *The Jungle*.

While Paton was in London during the winter of 1950 working on the script for the film of *Cry, the Beloved Country*, he was accorded the signal honor of being invited to preach a sermon at St. Paul's Cathedral, only the second layman ever to do so. He also gave a similar address at Oxford, Cambridge, and Birmingham.

When the film version of *Cry, the Beloved Country* opened in South Africa, it had three premieres. The proceeds from the first showing, which was attended by the wealthy whites of Natal, were donated, at Paton's request, to help build a settlement house for the treatment of tuberculosis among Africans. The guests of honor at the second premiere, held in Johannesburg, were South Africa's Prime Minister D.F. Malan and his wife, Maria-Anne. She turned to Paton and asked, "Surely, Mr. Paton, you don't really think things are like that?" Paton gently explained to her that he had lived and worked in a South African reformatory for thirteen years, and that indeed things really were like that. Paton flew to London for the third premiere, but following its opening there, interest in the film soon faded.

Too Late the Phalarope

After the resounding success of *Cry, the Beloved Country*, Paton resigned from Diepkloof to concentrate on writing. He and Dorrie spent the next few years in a seacoast village, walking the beach, swimming, and waiting for inspiration for the next novel. Thinking of its plot however, was not so easy for Paton as imagining the story of *Cry, the Beloved Country* had been. Finally, in 1951 he read a newspaper account that furnished him the kernel for his story. The article reported the trial of a white policeman whose duty it was to uphold the Immorality Act forbidding any sexual relations between whites and Africans. The policeman had not only not upheld the law, he had himself engaged in such a relationship. He would not have been found out had he not visited the African woman repeatedly. Even as Paton read the article, he knew he had found the pivotal theme for his next novel.

Later that year Paton was able to settle into writing the novel, *Too Late the Phalarope*, when he went off to a hotel in the quiet town of Falmouth in the southeast corner of England, taking a break from his work in London with Korda, filming *Cry, the Beloved Country*. Once well begun, the writing of his second novel continued steadily upon his return to London.

Too Late the Phalarope, like *Cry, the Beloved Country*, is based in part on his own life. For instance, Tante Sophie, the narrator and character most sympathetic to the policeman-protagonist, Pieter, is based on his beloved paternal grandmother. It takes its title from a subtheme he well knew, a father-son conflict. For too many years the father does not understand his son's sensitivity exemplified in his love of birds. When the father finally shows an interest in the phalarope, a seabird that nests inland, it is too late.

The novel's main theme is the downfall of that son, a white policeman, a small town hero and rugby player, Pieter Van Vlaanderen, who sleeps with a black woman while his own wife is out of town. Despite his efforts to put the incident behind him by means of prayer and self-discipline, he does not. The woman blackmails him, and he goes to see her one last time. Unable to keep his resolve not to sleep with her, he is trapped through a ruse by a white man, a jealous coworker in a lesser position. With the inevitability of Greek tragedy, Pieter is arrested, tried, and jailed, and his family is ruined.

Paton feared his second novel might not be well received, often an author's fate after rave reviews of a first book. He had no need to worry, though. Published in 1953, *Too Late the Phalarope* at once received acclaim. In Paton's homeland, Geoffrey Durrant wrote in the *Natal Witness*, "It is a book to be read here and now, especially in South Africa." Although Alfred Kazin in the *New York Times* Book Review considered it "less satisfactory" than *Cry, the Beloved Country*, other reviewers said it was "even more impressive" and "surpassed" Paton's first novel. The *Christian Science Monitor* said *Too Late the Phalarope* told "in terms of simple dignity and great power the ageless story of man's conflict with evil." In addition, in America it immediately became the Book of the Month Club selection, guaranteeing its financial success.

REACTION TO APARTHEID

In conflict with Paton's desire to write was his increasing concern over the political climate in South Africa. The Nationalist party had gained control of the nation's government in 1948. Under the Nationalists, more and more laws passed to restrict coloreds and black people in where they could live, where they could travel, and who they could associate with. Political power was restricted until eventually the right to vote was taken away from all but whites. Deeply disturbed, Paton curtailed his writing to become a voice against these policies, collectively known as apartheid.

Frustrated that no political party was willing to resist the Nationalists by peaceful means, in 1953 Paton helped found, fund, and lead a new, multiracial Liberal party. Although the Liberal party never won an elected office, Paton believed its role, "to do the best of things in the worst of times," was valuable, since its presence helped keep hope alive among South Africa's blacks, coloreds, and liberal whites.

As time went on, the government grew ever more repressive. Among the practices Paton and other Liberal party members found most objectionable was banning, a sentence that forbade the banned person from being quoted or from meeting with more than one person at a time, making most contact with others difficult or impossible. Other measures legalized placing citizens under house arrest and suspended the right of persons accused of certain crimes to a trial by jury. Many of Paton's fellow Liberals were arrested or banned, sometimes for ten years, and more and more left South Africa to avoid such a fate.

The Patons were neither arrested nor banned, but for fifteen years the security police were part of Paton's life. Paton was followed wherever he went, his phone was tapped, his passport was withheld, and personal property destroyed.

Despite the harassment, Paton attended Liberal party meetings all around Natal to boost morale among members and to promote the Party's program of nonviolent campaigning for equality. In essays he wrote for the Liberal party's publication, *Contact*, Paton promoted the party's ideals of equality for all racial groups in South Africa. Paton's efforts on behalf of the Liberals were abruptly sidelined, however, in 1968. In that year the Nationalist government prohibited any public meeting by people of different races, which effectively prevented the Liberal party from functioning, since by its very nature it was a multiracial organization. As each chapter held its last meeting, Paton attended and encouraged members to keep faith in their goals of a just society where everyone would be able to vote.

FREEDOM AWARD AND OTHER HONORS

In addition to his political activities at home, Paton had many invitations to go abroad for speaking engagements and other occasions. In 1960 he went to New York to accept from Freedom House the Freedom Award for his Liberal party work. Freedom House, the oldest human rights organization in the United States, founded in 1941 by Eleanor Roosevelt to honor proponents of democratic values and opponents of dictatorship, had given its first Freedom Award in 1943 and had honored such leaders as British Prime Minister Winston Churchill and Presidents Franklin D. Roosevelt and Dwight D. Eisenhower. The occasion honoring Paton was illustrious with congratulations sent from President Eisenhower, and so many literary and political figures wanting to attend that many had to be turned away.

Paton's Freedom Award trip, however, proved to be his last for some time. When his plane landed back in Johannesburg, the customs officials took his passport and did not return it. For over ten years, he refused to ask the government for its return because he felt it would be unfair for him to be allowed to travel abroad while many of his friends were in jail for no specified reason

TALES FROM A TROUBLED LAND

While Paton continued to be a voice for the liberal cause, he was also able to devote some of his energy to creative writing. In 1961 a book of his short stories was published, titled in the United States *Tales from a Troubled Land,* and in England, *Debbie, Go Home.* In one story, "A Drink in the Passage," a prize-winning African sculptor is invited home by a white admirer. Once home, though, the white man cannot bring himself to invite a black man inside, so, embarrassed, they drink a cocktail in the hallway. In "Debbie, Go Home," a mixed race girl wants to go to a debutante ball where she will shake hands with a white administrator. Her father is against her going. He considers the ceremony demeaning, as no other time in her life would the administrator be willing to shake hands with her. All the stories are poignant and told in Paton's clear, sparse prose.

Following the book's publication, the *New York Herald Tribune* referred to Paton as that rare thing, a writer "with an unfaltering social conscience who is also an artist." Several dramatists took an interest in converting stories from the collection into dramas, and with one, Krishna Shaw, Paton wrote *Sponono,* a play based on three of the stories he had written from his Diepkloof experience.

ANNE HOPKINS PATON

The 1960s were particularly difficult for Paton because his wife was ill for several years with emphysema, caused by smoking. Following Dorrie's death in 1967, a profound sense of grief enveloped Paton. He fell into depression and heavy whiskey drinking. His friends invited him for dinners, his sons, pitying him, invited him to go live with them. The person who brought him back to a productive life, though, was someone a friend suggested he hire as his secretary, Anne Hopkins. She quickly brought organization and order to his life and protected him from callers, affording Paton the time to write. Anne encouraged Paton in his writing as well. *For You Departed*, a tribute to Dorrie, was one work that he produced with Anne's prodding. Paton's relationship with Anne soon deepened, and Paton and Anne married.

INTERNATIONAL SPEAKING ENGAGEMENTS

Paton gladly relied on Anne to make their travel arrangements once he resumed making trips abroad. For over ten years he had not asked his government for permission to travel outside South Africa. Eventually, though, he relented and asked for his passport when in 1971 Harvard asked him to speak at commencement and offered him an honorary doctorate. Other international speaking engagements followed, which provided Paton a forum for articulating his liberal ideals. During a lecture Paton gave at Yale in 1973, he said:

> By liberalism I don't mean the creed of any party or country. I mean a generosity of spirit, a tolerance of others, an attempt to comprehend otherness, a commitment to the rule of law, a high ideal of the worth and dignity of man, a repugnance for authoritarianism, and a love of freedom.

ACHIEVEMENTS

As he advanced in years, Paton continued to be productive, although he accepted fewer speaking engagements than he had in the past. When Paton was seventy-seven, Scribners published the first volume of his autobiography, *Toward the Mountain*. At age eighty-one he published his third novel, *Ah, But Your Land Is Beautiful*, based on South African politics. It was to be the first part of what he planned as a trilogy. But heart problems caused him to cancel that plan. When he was eighty-four and his energy and health were declining, he still wrote, wanting to finish writing his life's story. In January 1988 Paton turned eighty-five, and in February he put the finishing touches on the second volume of his autobiography, *Journey Continued*. In its conclusion, he wrote, "I am grateful that life made it possible for me to pursue a writing career."

In March he began to experience trouble swallowing. Surgery to remove a cancerous tumor in his esophagus was unsuccessful, and when pneumonia set in, his son Jonathan and his wife Anne, following the terms of Paton's living will, took him home where he died the next morning, April 12, 1988.

As soon as the news was announced, tributes began, the phone at the Paton home rang constantly, and bags of mail piled up. After a small private funeral ceremony April 16, Paton's body was cremated. Large memorial services followed, first in Pietermaritzburg, then in cathedrals in Johannesburg, Cape Town, Washington, D.C., and London. The final ceremony occurred in October when Anne, alone, sprinkled Paton's ashes alongside a path in his beloved garden.

Alan Paton's works live on as a tribute to an author who lived a life of service to the common man, to his country, and to his God. This is especially true of his masterpiece, *Cry, the Beloved Country*. During his lifetime alone, it sold 15 million copies in over twenty languages including English, German, French, Afrikaans, and Zulu. Paton had regularly given to charitable purposes from his first novel's royalties, privately financing the education of many black people in several African countries. In his will he set up a trust to provide for his grandchildren with future royalties from *Cry, the Beloved Country*.

Paton's biographer, Peter Alexander, who had been a student of Jonathan at the University of Witwatersrand, eloquently sums up Alan Paton's achievements:

> His was the full and fortunate life of a profoundly talented man, as his range of careers suggests: teacher, prison reformer, writer, and politician. As a writer he will be read as long as the English language is read, for *Cry, the Beloved Country* is a great novel. . . .
>
> His prescription for the sharing of power, his urging of constitutional talks between the opposed sides, have proved since his death uncannily prophetic. . . . And his abiding faith that his country would in time be able to work out its problems should remain an inspiration and a source of hope. . . .
>
> He maintained . . . affirmation of the worth and dignity of the individual. . . . His Christian creed was . . . to uphold human rights . . . , to lift the downtrodden; and to promote a common society in opposition to the polarization of apartheid. He glorified God in loving his fellows . . . and had faith in the decency, tolerance, and humanity of the common man. . . .
>
> His was a life lived to the full, and lived unstintingly. He fought the good fight to the end; he ran the race to the finish; he kept the faith.

CHARACTERS AND PLOT

CHARACTERS

Stephen Kumalo. Kumalo is the humble *umfundisi,* or pastor, in the village of Ndotsheni. He is kind, devout, and compassionate; he is vulnerable to being duped but is also intelligent and learns from experience. In the novel Kumalo makes two journeys: The first, the physical round-trip from his peaceful but desolate village of Ndotsheni to the big city, Johannesburg, to search for his younger sister and his son, is a planned trip. The other, a journey of faith, is unplanned. Kumalo sets out for Johannesburg grounded in his faith. But after he learns that his sister and son are both involved in crime, that his son is a murderer even, and that his brother has become corrupt, it seems to Kumalo that God has abandoned him. His journey of faith, however, is ultimately a round-trip as well since his faith in God is restored by what he perceives to be answers to his prayers.

Absalom Kumalo. Absalom is the only son of Stephen Kumalo, the Anglican priest in the village of Ndotsheni. Absalom goes to Johannesburg to search for his aunt, Gertrude, but once there he falls into bad company. Although Absalom initially shows no remorse for murdering Arthur Jarvis, his redeeming quality is that he tells the truth and admits that it was he who committed the crime.

James Jarvis. Jarvis is the father of Arthur Jarvis, the man Absalom Kumalo murders. As it happens, he also is the farmer whose land overlooks the village of Ndotsheni. He experiences a conversion from being simply a respected, successful farmer who treats his black workers decently but with no particular concern to a man who involves himself with them and gives generously to promote the welfare of black Africans. Jarvis's change of heart comes as a result of finding his son's manuscripts, in which Arthur wrote movingly of the difficulties faced by blacks in South Africa.

Arthur Jarvis. Although Arthur does not engage in dialogue with any of the other characters in the novel, he still functions as a main character. Indirectly, he affects the plot not only because he is the murder victim but also because of the influence he has on his father through his essays, which the elder Jarvis reads after his son's death. At the time of his murder, Arthur is a well-respected member of his community and is considered likely to become a member of South Africa's parliament.

Theophilus Msimangu. Msimangu is Kumalo's companion in his search for Absalom. Like Kumalo, Msimangu is an Anglican priest. He stays by Kumalo's side during Absalom's trial. As Book II in the novel closes, Msimangu makes his final appearance when he hosts a farewell party for Kumalo and his family. When Msimangu announces his plan to enter a monastery, he gives all of his earthly savings to Kumalo.

Gertrude. Gertrude is Stephen Kumalo's much younger sister, who has left Ndotsheni for Johannesburg. When Kumalo receives a letter from a fellow priest in Johannesburg saying that Gertrude is very sick, he travels to the city to see her. Kumalo soon finds that Gertrude has become a prostitute and has borne an illegitimate son.

John Kumalo. John Kumalo is Stephen's younger brother. Materially successful, John Kumalo displays many of the effects of the corrupting influence of the big city.

Matthew Kumalo. Matthew is John Kumalo's son and has become involved in burglary. He is involved in the break-in that ends with Absalom Kumalo's killing of Arthur Jarvis.

John Pafuri. Pafuri is the third man involved in the murder of Arthur Jarvis. Although the police initially believe that Pafuri is the one who killed Jarvis, Absalom Kumalo decides to admit to the murder himself.

Father Vincent. Father Vincent is a white Anglican priest who befriends Stephen Kumalo upon his arrival in Johannesburg. It is Father Vincent's reminder to Kumalo that God does not abandon people that sets in motion Kumalo's spiritual renewal.

Absalom's Girlfriend. Referred to in the novel only as "the girl," Absalom Kumalo's girlfriend is pregnant with his child. Eventually, she marries Absalom in jail and thereafter accompanies Stephen Kumalo back to Ndotsheni.

THE PLOT: BOOK I

Cry, the Beloved Country opens in the South African village of Ndotsheni. The surrounding hills are green, but in the valley the soil is dry and eroded. Women, children, and the elderly try to scratch out a living. The men and young people are gone, having moved to the cities in search of work.

Humble sixty-year-old village priest Stephen Kumalo receives a letter from another priest, Theophilus Msimangu, telling Kumalo that his sister Gertrude is very ill and asking him to come to Johannesburg. He sets out the next morning, gripped by fear of the unknown city and, even more, by fear for his son Absalom, who went to the city some time before to find Gertrude. Neither has written nor returned to Ndotsheni. In addition, Kumalo has been asked to inquire after the whereabouts of a fellow villager's daughter.

As soon as he reaches the city with its bewildering traffic, Kumalo is duped out of some of his meager money by a young man pretending to buy him a bus ticket. That night, after dinner at the Mission House, where black and white priests dine together, Msimangu tells Kumalo the sad news that Gertrude sells liquor and works as a prostitute. He also tells Kumalo that she has been in prison repeatedly. Kumalo also learns that his brother John has left the church, owns a carpenter's shop, and is a politician. Msimangu takes Kumalo to Mrs. Lithebe, who has a small, clean room for him to stay in.

The next day Msimangu and Kumalo go to the nearby slum known as Claremont, where Gertrude lives. Msimangu waits while Kumalo calls on Gertrude. That afternoon Kumalo sends a truck for Gertrude's few belongings, and Lithebe takes in Gertrude and her young son. Kumalo feels encouraged that in one day the tribe is beginning to be restored. He buys his sister a new red dress and white turban as well as clothes and wooden blocks for her son.

The next morning Kumalo and Msimangu go to John Kumalo's carpentry shop. There, John talks of being a "somebody" in Johannesburg and of how whites take advantage of black miners by paying low wages. John looks up the address of the factory where he says his son, Matthew, and Absalom work.

Their search for Absalom goes on day after day, leading Kumalo and Msimangu from one section of Johannesburg to another, with worse news at every stop. One person they speak with, Mrs. Ndela, indicates that Absalom has fallen into bad company, saying she did not like his friends. Their next lead points the men toward the community of Alexandra, eleven miles away. Kumalo and Msimangu initially plan to take a bus, but they later decide to walk when they learn there is a boycott to protest a proposed hike in bus fares. In Alexandra they hear that Absalom and his friends seem to be dealing in stolen goods.

Kumalo and Msimangu's search eventually leads to a reformatory. There, they learn that Absalom was released early for good behavior. They also learn that he has a girlfriend who is pregnant and that he seems to really care for her and the unborn child. They go to see the girl, but she says Absalom has been gone for days and has not been at work.

That night at the Mission House, the priests read the headline "Murder in Parkwold. Well-Known City Engineer Shot Dead. Assailants Thought to be Natives." Kumalo says he knows the victim's father, James Jarvis, his own white neighbor on the rich farm above Ndotsheni, and he remembers the victim, Arthur Jarvis, when he was a "small bright boy." To Msimangu, Kumalo confides his worst fear—that Absalom is the murderer. The next day Absalom's girlfriend tells Kumalo and Msimangu that the police have just left her home.

A few days later Kumalo learns that the murderer is his son. He breaks the news to his brother as gently as he can that Matthew Kumalo and another young man were accomplices in the crime. They go to see their sons in jail. In a torturous scene, Absalom gives no real answers to his father's questions about why he committed the crime. When the brothers meet afterward, John disregards the truth and cruelly says he will get a lawyer because there is no proof that his own son and the other young man were at the crime scene.

An anguished scene occurs between Kumalo, now at his lowest point spiritually, and a white priest, Father Vincent. Kumalo laments that he and Absalom's mother had no warning of their son's going astray and that his son seems only to pity himself and does not seem to repent of the evil he has done. Father Vincent commands him to stop, to go pray, and to rest. Father Vincent also reminds Kumalo that God does not abandon one and tells Kumalo that his most important duty now is to help his son amend his life.

Getting accustomed to the city, Kumalo goes alone to talk to Absalom's girlfriend. He discovers that she wants to marry

Absalom and would like to move to Ndotsheni. Kumalo then goes to see Absalom, and his son tells him that the other two young men have deserted him. Kumalo tells his son that he will be able to marry the girl, have a lawyer, and make his confession to Father Vincent, be absolved, and mend his ways.

When Kumalo meets the lawyer, Mr. Carmichael, he says he will take the case pro bono, or without pay. Carmichael says he thinks it best to let the judge and his assistants try the case without a jury. The lawyer will try to convince the judge that Absalom is telling the truth about his accomplices and that he shot Arthur Jarvis out of fear but that he had not intended to kill him.

Book II

Book II returns to the hills above Ndotsheni, this time to James Jarvis's prosperous farm. He is there when two policemen bring him news: At 1:30 that afternoon his son, Arthur, was fatally shot. Grief stricken, Jarvis and his wife fly to Johannesburg, where Jarvis learns of his son's deep commitment toward helping the natives.

In his son's study, Jarvis finds pictures of Abraham Lincoln and of the crucifixion of Jesus as well as myriad books and invitations, often for speaking engagements. He also reads his son's last manuscript, in which he wrote of the dilemma of whites in South Africa. These are people who want to behave as Christians, but their greed causes them to oppress black Africans.

Absalom's trial for Arthur Jarvis's murder begins. He testifies that during the break-in his friend Johannes Pafuri hit a servant with a bar and that he himself killed Jarvis. He reiterates that he had not intended to commit murder. He testifies further that when the police had come to him in search of Pafuri, he had told them of his own role in the crime and had shown them where he had hidden the revolver he had used. The court adjourns for the day. Stephen Kumalo trembles when he recognizes the father of the murdered man on the way out of the courtroom.

Jarvis again visits his son's study, where he reads a work Arthur wrote, "Private Essay on the Evolution of a South African." In his essay, Arthur tells how he, realizing his parents have taught him honesty, charity, and generosity but nothing about South Africa itself, has decided to devote his time and talents to doing what is right for all South Africans, whatever the cost.

At this point Kumalo decides to fulfill his promise to locate his fellow villager's daughter, and he goes to the home of Barbara Smith, who, he had been told, was the young woman's employer. It happens that Barbara is a cousin of Arthur Jarvis's and that the elder Jarvises are there visiting. When Jarvis answers the door, Kumalo drops his cane and hat and cannot look at him. Jarvis wants to know what is the matter, and when Kumalo says it is "the heaviest thing of all my days," Jarvis assures him he will not be angry when Kumalo explains. With greatest difficulty, Kumalo tells of Absalom's role in Arthur's death and expresses deep sorrow for the Jarvises, Arthur's widow, and the children. Jarvis asks if the priest remembers Arthur as a boy, and Kumalo says, "There was a brightness in him."

The court meets again. The judge sums up the case. Because he and his assistants agree that masks over part of the young men's faces made identification, even with a scar such as Pafuri has, uncertain, Matthew Kumalo and John Pafuri are found not guilty. However, the judge says he has a sacred duty to uphold the law, despite whether it is just; because he finds no extenuating circumstances, the judge pronounces Absalom guilty of murder and sentences him to be hanged.

On the family's final visit to Absalom, he and his young girlfriend are married by Father Vincent in the prison chapel. Absalom gives his small savings to his father to use for raising the coming child. Hearing that his father plans to return the next day to Ndotsheni, Absalom breaks down, sobbing, clinging to his father's legs so tightly that it takes two guards to pull him off.

Meanwhile, as the Jarvises say goodbye to Arthur's brother-in-law, John Harrison, who, along with Arthur, has been active in helping an African boys' club. Jarvis, whose attitude toward blacks has been changed by his son's writings, amazes Harrison by giving him one thousand pounds for the club.

That night Msimangu gives a farewell party for Kumalo at Lithebe's home. After dinner and speeches, Msimangu announces that he has decided to enter a monastery. Renouncing worldly possessions, he gives Kumalo all of his savings, a sum of money greater than Kumalo has ever had at one time. The next morning Kumalo goes to Gertrude's room to awaken her for the trip. Her son is there, but she has disappeared.

BOOK III

As Kumalo arrives home from Johannesburg with Gertrude's son and Absalom's wife, the villagers call out joyful greetings, send up a Zulu cry, dance, and sing to welcome him. He joins in on a hymn. Absalom's wife stands in wonder. Kumalo prays for protection from starvation, for rain, for all who are there, especially for the family members he has brought home, and for Absalom. Later that night Kumalo shows his wife the money Msimangu gave him.

Kumalo prays regularly for the restoration of Ndotsheni and goes to see both the chief and the school's headmaster, but they have no idea of how to help. While Kumalo works on the church accounts, a small boy, Arthur Jarvis's son, comes to visit, hoping to practice speaking Zulu. When the boy asks for a glass of cold milk, he learns there is no milk in the village, that the people are so poor that in one family a child is dying of starvation. That night a friend of Kumalo's brings milk for the preschoolers and says it will continue to come from Jarvis until the villagers' cows are able to give milk again.

Letters come. In one, Absalom's lawyer says there will be no mercy; the execution day has been set. In another letter, Absalom says a priest is preparing him for death. Absalom says that if he could be back in Ndotsheni, he would never leave again.

As a storm builds over the valley, a magistrate arrives by car and Jarvis comes on horseback. These two men work together on plans for an irrigation dam that will serve the farmers. The magistrate leaves, but Jarvis takes cover with Kumalo in the church, the tin roof of which leaks so badly that only with difficulty does each man find a dry spot. When the storm abates, Jarvis asks if the court has commuted Absalom's sentence. Kumalo shows him the letter from the lawyer. Jarvis says he will remember Absalom on the day of his execution. Again, their mutual sorrow has drawn the two fathers close.

A young man, Napoleon Letsisi, arrives in the village, hired by Jarvis as an agricultural demonstrator to teach the villagers better farming methods to restore the fertility of the valley. The demonstrator introduces changes such as irrigation, contour plowing, better seed for planting, and a kraal to confine cows so their dung can be used for fertilizer. The demonstrator warns Kumalo that the restoration of the soil will support only those living there now; in a future generation, some people will still have to leave. Even so, the restoration is a godsend.

The villagers learn that Mrs. Jarvis has died and they carefully prepare a wreath for her funeral service. Kumalo sends a boy on a horse to deliver the wreath and a sympathy note. Meanwhile, the bishop in the area comes to confirm young boys and girls in Kumalo's church. Afterwards, the bishop meets alone with Kumalo and advises him to leave the village. While Kumalo is suppressing his grief over this order, the boy who delivered the wreath brings a thank-you letter from Jarvis, who also says he wants to build a new church in Ndotsheni. "This is from God," Kumalo says of the letter. The bishop, seeing the letter and hearing how the villagers have welcomed their priest back and accepted Absalom's wife, tells Kumalo to stay.

On the eve of Absalom's execution, Kumalo goes to the mountaintop for an all-night vigil. On his way he meets Jarvis riding horseback. Jarvis thanks Kumalo for the beautiful wreath and sympathizes with Kumalo. They talk about Jarvis's grandson and the brightness in him, and part with "Go well, Stay well" wishes.

Kumalo keeps vigil, prays, falls asleep, and eats and drinks what his wife has sent. He wonders if his son's fear leaves room for repentance. Kumalo alternately prays hard and checks the sky to the east. When the sun is about to come over the horizon—the time of executions—he stands and grasps his hands before him. The sun rises.

Cry, the Beloved Country ends with thoughts of when fear will leave the hearts of Africans, a time that is "a secret."

CHAPTER 1

Themes in *Cry, the Beloved Country*

READINGS ON
CRY, THE BELOVED COUNTRY

The Disintegration of Tribal Society

Harold Reeves Collins

The following excerpt from a 1953 article by Harold Reeves Collins focuses on South Africa in the 1940s when the social structure of whole tribes disintegrated, the result of young people and married men going to work in the mines and cities, away from the moral order and control of the tribe. Collins taught at Kent State University in Ohio and wrote several articles on African literature and education.

Cry, the Beloved Country is a "story of comfort in desolation." We shall observe that the desolation consists not so much in the crowded native reserves, or the ruin of the reserved land by erosion and overcropping, or the absence of the young men drawn to the mines, or the frightful living conditions of the town natives—terrible as these afflictions are—but in the loss of the old African moral order that gave purpose and meaning to African lives. . . .

We recall that the Zulu preacher's sister Gertrude goes to Johannesburg to find her husband and becomes a prostitute there, that his son Absalom, sent to the great city to find the sister, falls among evil companions, becomes a thief and a murderer. Arthur Jarvis, whom Absalom murders, has been a prominent *kaffirboetie* (or friend of the natives). His bereaved father finds among his son's manuscripts what seems to be an address on native crime, ironically, an explanation of the high incidence of crime among the Africans in the towns:

> The old tribal system was, for all its violence and savagery, for all its superstition and witchcraft, a moral system. Our natives today produce criminals and prostitutes and drunkards, not because it is their nature to do so, but because their simple system of order and tradition and convention has been destroyed. It has been destroyed by the impact of our own civilization. Our civilization has therefore the inescapable duty to set up another system of order and tradition and convention.

Excerpted from Harold Reeves Collins, "*Cry, the Beloved Country* and the Broken Tribe," *College English*, vol. 14, no. 7, April 1953. Copyright © 1953 The National Council of Teachers of English.

Indeed, one of the most important effects of European civilization in Africa is the deterioration and breakdown of the old African cultures and the consequent breakdown in African personalities. In the past our observation of the striking differences between these native African cultures and those of the Western world, and, perhaps even more, our feelings of racial superiority, have blinded us to the fact of the moral force of the old order. Now we begin to understand what has been happening. In the twentieth century, especially outside the reservations, in the mining compounds, the squatting grounds on the white men's farms, and the native slum "locations," Africans have been "detribalized," as the technical term has it. They have been losing the old moral standards without assuming, or being able to assume, those of the white men. Like Absalom and Matthew Kumalo, they have become social derelicts almost completely without moral guidance of any sort and, naturally enough, criminals.

Before the tribes were broken, the Africans had a good deal of moral guidance in their traditional religions. [According to Edwin Smith,] an experienced missionary and expert on the West African peoples,

> The behavior of Africans is not left to uncharted freedom, but is governed by a system of rules and regulations, so extensive, so complicated, that Europeans who study it stand amazed, and are tempted to declare the Africans to be the slaves of tribal custom.... The riotous instincts are restrained by forces that are not of this tangible sphere. In other words, the ethics of the Africans, their customary morality is grounded in their religion.

In the Kumalos' Zululand the old African religion has gone forever, though witchcraft has not. Absalom and the pitiful young girl he lives with are "Church of England," but their religion has no real hold on them. Their morality is not grounded in Christianity, certainly.

Anyone who wants to learn about detribalization would do well to consult *Africa*, the journal of the International Institute of African Languages and Cultures, which specializes in studies of the problems of culture contact. In this journal we find anthropological studies that confirm Paton's view of the broken tribe. For instance, Miss Ellen Hellman's "Native Life in a Johannesburg Slum Yard" is a study of the conduct of Africans in an environment rather like Claremont, Alexandra, and Orlando, where Gertrude, Absalom, and Matthew Kumalo are corrupted. Her conclusions are precisely those of Arthur Jarvis—and Alan Paton:

In the drive to town families are separated from their kinfolk
and form isolated groups in town. The restraints of tribal discipline do not affect the urban native, and no substitute discipline
has, as yet, emerged from out of the chaotic welter of transition.
The old sanctions have lost their force and the sanctions which
order European life are not applicable to native life.

Presuming that Europeans are controlled by public opinion,
law, and the precepts of Christianity, Miss Hellman points
out [in *Africa*, VIII (January 1935), p. 60] that for these
Africans there is "no body of public opinion," that conviction
and imprisonment carry no social stigma because the criminal sanction has been applied to trivial misdemeanors, and
that the great majority of the slum yard natives have "tacitly
rejected Christianity."

For Absalom Kumalo there was "no body of public opinion"
beyond the promptings of such unimproving acquaintances as
his cousin Matthew, Johannes Pafuri, and Baby Mkise. Such acquaintances would not be in much awe of penal sanctions, and
who can blame them, really, when an African can be arrested
for some irregularity in his passes? It would seem that Absalom
has "tacitly rejected Christianity" and taken his uncle's measure
of his Christian father—"a white man's dog."

In a culture contact study of a group of Africans in north-
western Rhodesia, Audrey I. Richards gives a series of case
histories of detribalized persons. The history of Jackie Bil-
tong is representative, and Jackie reminds us of the Kumalo
boys, though the district in which he lives is an isolated one
where the introduction of taxes and the money economy is
just beginning to send the men to the distant labor centers,
the points from which white influences radiate. Jackie's father, sacked from a job as a cook, went to the mines and took
his son with him, and the woman he lived with brought Jackie
up. Jackie is "smartly dressed" but somewhat disreputable and
irresponsible. "Caught for pilfering," he is living on food
cooked by his friend's mother and a relative of his mother. Re-
cently he made ten shillings digging a garden for the local
prostitute, and has spent the money on "clothes and beer"; he
says he will "pay back friend and look for tax later on."

The African novels of Joyce Cary, written out of his seven
years' experience as a political officer in Nigeria, and those
of Elspeth Huxley, an expert on African colonial affairs and
a former Kenya settler, throw considerable light on the
process of detribalization. Cary's novels are crowded with

strayed souls, tribeless Africans free of the old African sanctions and not controlled by European sanctions. We observe what the breaking of the tribes means in terms of the disorganization of African personalities. . . .

Cary's Africans, like Gertrude, Absalom, and Matthew Kumalo, get into trouble when they leave the tribe and enter the white man's world. Henry in *An American Visitor* (1933) is a "smooth operator" who finally opens a store in the minefields and does a splendid trade in condemned and slightly blown tinned meats, secondhand caps and trousers, aphrodisiacs, smuggled gin, and abortion drugs. Ajaki in *Mister Johnson* (1947) is a cash-drawer thief. The title character of that novel is a first-rate grafter, extorting his own personal tolls on a new road and embezzling treasury funds. Like Absalom Kumalo, he inadvertently murders a man who surprises him in amateurish housebreaking. . . .

Although District Officer Bewsher [in *An American Visitor*] has tried manfully to protect the Birri from all white in-

---

DESTROYING THE TRIBAL SYSTEM

According to Arthur Jarvis, a character in Cry, the Beloved Country, *it was acceptable for white South Africans to allow the destruction of the tribal system thinking it was inevitable, or to try to preserve the tribal system by segregation—but only to the extent that white people did this out of ignorance. Then, because whites did not provide a suitable alternative to the tribal system, their actions lost all moral justification.*

It was permissible when we discovered gold to bring labour to the mines. It was permissible to build compounds and to keep women and children away from the towns. It was permissible as an experiment, in the light of what we knew. But in the light of what we know now, with certain exceptions, it is no longer permissible. It is not permissible for us to go on destroying family life when we know that we are destroying it. . . .

It is not permissible to add to one's possessions if these things can only be done at the cost of other men. Such development has only one true name, and that is exploitation. It might have been permissible in the early days of our country, before we became aware of its cost, in the disintegration of native community life, in the deterioration of native family life, in poverty, slums and crime. But now that the cost is known, it is no longer permissible. . . .

It was permissible to allow the destruction of a tribal system that impeded the growth of the country. It was permissible to

fluences, even missionary activity, the Birri elders observe the breaking-up of the old culture; in their passionate regret for the old order passing away, they make Bewsher their scapegoat. They blame him for the "misfortunes of the time" and the "collapse of their own authority, of all decency and good behavior."

When malcontent Africans rebel against the whites, they merely give the *coup de grâce* [death blow] to their native society. Bewsher is unable to prevent a mining company from encroaching on tribal land. The Birri, feeling that they have been betrayed to the "interests," kill their benefactor and revolt. In a punitive expedition against this small, backward Nigerian tribe, only thirty natives are killed, but the old society is broken beyond repair. The old cultural forms, already badly undermined, collapse completely under the pressure of routine military operations: "The old patriarchal government disappeared and the people became a mob. Large numbers of the young men drifted away, even during

believe that its destruction was inevitable. But it is not permissible to watch its destruction, and to replace it by nothing, or by so little, that a whole people deteriorates, physically and morally.

The old tribal system was, for all its violence and savagery, for all its superstition and witchcraft, a moral system. Our natives today produce criminals and prostitutes and drunkards, not because it is their nature to do so, but because their simple system of order and tradition and convention has been destroyed. It was destroyed by the impact of our own civilization. Our civilization has therefore an inescapable duty to set up another system of order and tradition and convention.

It is true that we hoped to preserve the tribal system by a policy of segregation. That was permissible. But we never did it thoroughly or honestly. We set aside one-tenth of the land for four-fifths of the people. Thus we made it inevitable, and some say we did it knowingly, that labour would come to the towns. We are caught in the toils of our own selfishness.

No one wishes to make the problem seem smaller than it is. No one wishes to make its solution seem easy. No one wishes to make light of the fears that beset us. But whether we be fearful or no, we shall never, because we are a Christian people, be able to evade the moral issues.

Arthur Jarvis in *Cry, the Beloved Country*, 1948.

the campaign, to join the flotsam of wandering laborers and petty thieves in the neighboring provinces." After the "war" Bewsher's successor finds it expedient to bring in a mission and a mining company to integrate the mob, make something like a society of it.

> Desperately anxious to protect his Birri from the disruptive force of white civilization, Bewsher invents a synthetic culture for them—a hodgepodge of private property, co-operative marketing, and a neo-pagan religion which is the old creed and ritual with Christian ethics "pumped in." This intriguing scheme sleeps quietly in official files.

The tribeless Africans of the South African towns and cities belong to just such an improvised society. They are essentially a mob, and a mob rejecting the standards of white public opinion, white law, and Christianity.

In Elspeth Huxley's *Red Strangers* (1939) . . . the British "conquer" the Kikuyu easily enough. They muddle badly, however, when they undertake to rule a people they know so little about. They set up the head of the Warriors' Council as the responsible native official in the group, not knowing that the clan has always been governed by the Council of Elders. When the elders, shorn of their judicial power, no longer sit as the clan court, "Men steal and evade punishment, for the thieves no longer pay compensation." The Kikuyu never really understand just what is forbidden by the white men's law; the white men know nothing of traditional Kikuyu law. Because of language difficulties, justice is blind indeed. But even more outrageous from the native point of view, the "red strangers" force the proud young men, who ought to be warriors, to do portage, always considered "woman's work." There is a disquieting breakdown of parental discipline. One old father complains, "In your youth and mine we could not have insulted our fathers; we feared the wrath of the elders, and only our fathers could provide us with wives." Now the young men have no reason to fear the elders, and they can go to work for the white men and earn the bride price themselves.

THE TRIBE AS TEACHER AND CONSCIENCE BUILDER

The missionaries, who "teach their magic to children," even encourage the children to "speak to God," undermine the authority of the *mundu-mugu*, the witch doctor—an authority vital to the community. Besides conducting the sacrifices that rid his people of the evil spirits causing their misfor-

tunes and their ailments and the religious observances involved in the worship of the ancestors, he instructs the young
men in the responsibilities of adult life in the clan. He is the
guardian of that "system of order and tradition and convention" of which Arthur Jarvis speaks.

Huxley's *mundu-mugu* describes this system himself in a
talk to an initiation group:

> Thus some threads link a man to his father's clan and others
> bind him to his circumcision brothers. Different ties bind
> him to the elders who rule the country and administer the
> law. All these threads come together to form a web, and that
> web is the Kikuyu people. . . . So a man must fulfill his oblig-
> ations as readily as he uses his privileges; so he must fight
> with courage and labor with devotion; so he must beget chil-
> dren and respect the elders; and in all things he must act with
> justice and obey the law.[1]

Such doctrine would have been good for Absalom Kumalo. Yes, but we cannot blame Stephen Kumalo because he
has not adequately replaced the witch doctor or "circumcision father" of the old times, nor think poorly of Christianity
because it has not done the work of the old African religion.
Taxes, the money economy, and the flashier attractions of
European civilization have sent the young men to the labor
centers, where they live among indifferent whites and alien
Africans, in squalid slums where corrupting temptations are
strong. They live in such environments as have produced
crime among all races, all nationalities.

What happens when the "threads" bind no longer, when the
web is broken, is made plain in the behavior of two young
Kikuyu, Karanja and Karioki, who are no longer bound by the
old customs, as Gertrude, Absalom, and Matthew Kumalo were
not. "I hid behind the door and struck his head with an iron
tool. . . . I did not kill him. [He was luckier than Absalom.] . . . A
man of experience was with me; he had iron tools with which
to open the safe." The young man who describes his adventure
thus is thoroughly emancipated from the old ways of tribal life.
Karanja and Karioki buy bicycles and European hats and
shoes, the outward and obvious signs of white men's magic and
puissance. Then, since it seems to these amateur criminals
smart and progressive to adopt the white men's religion, they

1. In Beryl Markham's autobiography, *West with the Night* [Boston, 1942, p. 148], a
Nandi servant explains to Miss Markham that his circumcision father had told him
"how a man should live his life, keeping his voice soft and his anger sheathed until
there was just need of it," what a man should eat, and how he should love "so that he
remains a man and is yet not like a bull in the herd or a hyena clawing at a feast."

set out for the nearest mission. They are in rather a hurry, for Karanja has contracted a bad *thalu* from a prostitute in town and needs to take the cure in the mission hospital.

One might suppose that a good European education would repair the damage to the African personality wrought by the breaking of the tribe, would be the salvation of young men like Karanja, Karioki, and the Kumalo boys. In Huxley's *The Walled City* (1948) we learn what really happens to the educated African. The Nigerian Benjamin Morris, a graduate of an English university and an editor of a small African newspaper, is hurt because the white road foreman and the white sanitary engineer pass him on the street without so much as a nod. It shames him to be patronized by "such inferior persons, who could not explain the differences between the Stoic and Epicurean schools, or outline the quantum theory." Because the Europeans are aloof, Benjamin is acutely unhappy. He loses interest in his liberal magazines from England, relapses into some of the old African superstitions, and prints the most shameless canards against the government. As long as the whites refuse to accord respect to the educated African, the very best European education cannot integrate the African personality. . . .

Certainly Paton has been scrupulously fair on the "native problem." His view on the injustice of keeping Africans unskilled to support white supremacy, of developing natural resources at the expense of the welfare of African laborers, of destroying the old African tribal system and letting the Africans deteriorate physically and morally (as dramatically presented in Arthur Jarvis' address on native crime), are set in the context of the old Zulu preacher's agonizing discoveries of the degeneration of his son. Now the African novels and nonfiction sources referred to here have shown that such degeneration is commonplace [in the 1930s and 1940s] in Africa. Moreover, none of the characters in the novel, not even Arthur Jarvis or the kindly Mr. Msimangu, has a pat and easy solution for the afflictions of South Africa. Paton honestly renders the troubled complexity of the situation—the bewilderment of the whites and Africans caught up in the baffling problems of race conflict, the confusion, the cross-purposes, the frustration of men of good will of both races. *Cry, the Beloved Country* does what no discursive work in political science, sociology, economics, or anthropology could ever do; it makes us understand "how it feels" to be a South African [in the 1940s].

Fear Pervades *Cry, the Beloved Country*

Tony Morphet

Tony Morphet has published articles on both education and literature. When he was a Senior Lecturer
at the Centre for Extra-Mural Studies, University of
Cape Town, he wrote the article from which the following excerpt is taken. In this essay, Morphet identifies fear as the emotion that lies at the heart of *Cry, the
Beloved Country.* Morphet praises Paton and several
characters he creates in the novel for meditating on
and trying to answer questions about fear in South
Africa—questions their country had not yet faced up to.

For the mainspring of his story we have his [Paton's] un-
equivocal statements that the origins of the story lie in an
"emotion".

The emotion most pervasively present in the story is un-
questionably fear. All forms of experience from the most immediate and simple to the most harrowing are shadowed by
the sense of fear. It is a powerful unifying force in the novel,
acting almost as a kind of connective tissue within which the
shapes and patterns of experience are lodged. There is a
fierce hidden irony in the role which fear takes on in the
story. It is the structural unifier, the common emotion felt
and shared by everyone and present in everything, but it is
also the destroyer, the cancer which eats away and breaks
down the will to do good. The medium in which the story
lives is itself destructive. Buried, I think, within this paradox
is part of the "mesmeric" power of the emotion Paton himself
experienced in writing. The origin of the fear is within the author, from where it gains its pervasive power. It is literally the
source of the story, which it sets going and whose progress it
shapes. The art of the novel arises out of the author's encounter and struggle with the pervasive presence of fear.

Excerpted from Tony Morphet, "Alan Paton: The Honour of Meditation," *English in
Africa*, vol. 10, no. 2, October 1983. Reprinted with permission from Rhodes University, South Africa.

To come to terms with Paton we need to understand a great deal more about his experience and understanding of fear. In the novel there are several layers of familiar and conventional meaning in his use of the word. There are simple specific fears: of strangers, of dangerous places, of bad news, of trouble; there are also more wide-ranging psychological fear states, of vulnerability, of loss, of loss of status, of failure. Beyond even these are radical fears: of uncertainty, of the future, of collective fate or destiny.

At the deepest level the poetic exploration of the fear state can be grasped most fully through the famous paragraph which gives the novel its title.

> Cry, the beloved country, for the unborn child that is the inheritor of our fear. Let him not love the earth too deeply. Let him not laugh too gladly when the water runs through his fingers, nor stand too silent when the setting sun makes red the veld with fire. Let him not be too moved when the birds of his land are singing, nor give too much of his heart to a mountain or a valley. For fear will rob him of all if he gives too much.

THE PARADOX OF FEAR

I take the paragraph as an irony-laden lament or prayer. The displacement of the prayer to the "unborn child" only intensifies the pressure of the meditation and the urgency of the wish. At its heart is Paton who wants desperately to be able himself to love the earth, to laugh gladly, to experience the wonder of the sunset. That wish grows out of his own experience of the thwarting or corrosion of a passional desire for the freedom of the self. The images of a free and boundless nature convey with great force the intensity of the desire. But the advice and counsel ("Let him not love") offered as the voice of prudence and restraint is, through the irony, bitterly given—out of necessity, as it were. The force of the argument beneath the poetry is that prudence and restraint are the means of survival in the face of the destructive power of fear. Without restraint, with the passional wish given full commitment, the self is utterly vulnerable. The scale of this vulnerability is too great to be brought directly into the writing and can only be obliquely stated: "fear will rob him *of all*".

The paragraph constructs, focuses and intensifies the paradox of fear mentioned earlier. In counselling prudence and restraint the structure affirms the passion and desire. Each commitment challenges the other. Fear brings the desire to life and the desire creates fear. The great brilliance of the paragraph, and it is the heart of the book, is that its strange poetic form keeps the full force of the contradiction alive and causes the terms and the emotions to pulse with intensity.

It is fair ... to ask how such a powerful nexus [series, connection] of feelings arises within an individual author—they are after all the reason for his *authority*—and in Paton's case there are at least two directions in which one may begin looking for an answer. [Paton's autobiography] *Towards the Mountain* provides evidence (though for this purpose it is insufficient) of an early childhood lived out between concealed private "ecstasy" and being kept "unspoiled from the world" by the "great number of moralities" of the parents. The roots of the feelings in *Cry, the Beloved Country* are undoubtedly here; but the other source of answers must surely lie in Paton's mature awareness of his situation in the history of his own society. In the quoted paragraph the lament calls for the country to cry for the unborn child—a strange call which unites the landscapes of nature and the hosts of unborn children just as it excludes both time and society. History and society are present in the text only in the word "fear". ...

There are several other places in the book where the same basic paradox finds expression, though inevitably they are less poetic and less intense in form. In all of them the expression is in terms of South African society and its history. Arthur Jarvis's unfinished speech is an obvious example:

> The truth is that our Christian civilisation is riddled through and through with dilemma. We believe in the brotherhood of man but we do not want it in South Africa. We believe that God endows men with diverse gifts, and that human life depends for its fullness on their employment and enjoyment, but we are afraid to explore this belief too deeply. We believe in help for the underdog but we want him to stay under .... The truth is that our civilisation is not Christian; it is a tragic compound of great ideal and fearful practice, of high assurance and desperate anxiety, of loving charity and fearful clutching of possessions.

Here the paradox becomes "dilemma" and "tragic compound" and the nexus expresses social conditions in a form which came to be identified as Paton's 'liberalism'. My argument about the central paragraph in substance is that behind the liberal social stance lies a far more profound and troubling experience of the meaning of South Africa.

"WHAT MUST I BE?"

. . . In the interests of clarifying my argument I would like to "decode" what I believe to be the major terms of this troubling experience. In the novel I think Paton meditates upon a question, looking not so much for specific answers to it but rather measuring and weighing the density and reach of the question. At its simplest the question is "What must I be to live in this place at this time?" In the conventional formulation the question is neither difficult nor troubling and it is asked many times and in many ways. The power of *Cry, the Beloved Country* is in the seriousness, fullness and openness with which that question is asked—every term is given its fullest possible resonance. "I" is the fully experienced mature personal self, integral and self-conscious; "be" is the encompassing existential term going beyond "doing", "believing" and "offering"; "live" carries the force of the passional desires present in the central matrix of the book as well as the painful difficulties of fear; "in this place at this time" holds the society and history which the novel so effectively evokes.

The novel is a meditative engagement with that question not as it is crudely phrased in my explanation but as it is felt by the author. Crucial to the meditation is the fact that its source is in a white man, a coloniser, present at the moment when the colonial society transforms its own history and fully enters a system much larger than itself. To the thinking and feeling white consciousness the society and its history are both his and not his. How much they are "not his", to what extent they are alien, hostile, ruined, is very much part of the burden of the question.

For that reason the meditation begins and ends in the consciousness of the most vulnerable of men. Not the hard, unexpectant, unillusioned man at the very base of a bitter and unfulfilling world, but a priest who intellectually, socially and in faith has come to expect some fulfilment of the Christian message in history. On him falls the full weight of the destructive force of the society. He can perceive and value the grace of ameliorative and reconstructive efforts but the facts of ruin occupy his mind. The meditation is cast in this form to create the confrontations between the author's consciousness and the old priest's experience. In a sense the question as I have put it—"What must I be to live in this place at this time?"—is put by the author to the priest, as well as to himself.

To the social questions—"What to do? How to organise? What to offer?"—*Cry, the Beloved Country* does offer answers. Msimangu, for example, is in many ways exemplary in showing what to do; the rural development scheme for Ndotsheni may be seen as a practical answer in reconciliation; the bus boycott is another answer in the form of mobilised power. Yet none of these comes close to answering the crucial personal issue at the heart of the book, and the novel provides nothing that can be considered an answer to that predicament. To say this is not in any way to limit Paton's achievement. Rather the opposite, when one sees the insubstantial lists of "styles" and "principles" and "attitudes" that most fiction recommends as resolutions for the same basic issue. It is Paton's strength that he stays with the question so deeply and so fully, living as he does in Kumalo's awareness.

The meditation produces no resolution. The vigil of Kumalo in the dawn is intensely moving but he is there at that moment precisely because that is when his own son is being hanged. It is the paradox relived in yet another set of terms and circumstances. Amid the vigil filled with the knowledge of the world and with the hopes for fulfilment there is the steady unremitting knowledge of the death of his son.

> That men should walk upright in the land where they were born, and be free to use the fruits of the earth, what was there evil in it? Yet men were afraid, with a fear that was deep, deep in the heart, a fear so deep that they hid their kindness, or brought it out with fierceness and anger, and hid it behind fierce and frowning eyes. They were afraid because they were so few.

TWO ATTACKS ON FEAR

The novel could provide no answer because there was no answer available in the society and its history. This was I think clearly understood by Paton and, as his subsequent actions show, he took definite steps to create possible answers. They were however steps of a very particular and surprising kind and in their uncompromising character and their scale they demonstrate louder than any words just how difficult such answers are.

The first notable step was the formation of the Liberal Party. The passage of time, the flood of commentary and plain fashion have largely obscured the extraordinary nature of this endeavour. What it amounted to at the time

(1953) was an attempt to establish, within the fear-ridden destructive world described in the novel, a party of people committed to a single fundamental politics—the politics of innocence. Members joining the party were implicitly asked to reconstitute their personal identity within a form which might be considered to precede the fall of South Africa into racist history. They were to be pre-capitalist, pre-colonial—in a way prehistoric, and relations between members were to be shaped by a pre-lapsarian vision. What is even more extraordinary is that the party could command the support and allegiance that it did. The interests on which it was founded lay completely outside time, history and society, and yet it drew to it a wide range of people of all colours and classes, all of whom shared a commitment to hope. For Paton the party held a very special significance. It was his attempt to encounter the terms of history and society without compromise and without fear. It was an attempt to answer the terrible paradox of the novel. If "the party" could be South Africa then the desire for freedom would no longer be attacked by fear. Passion and prudence would be one and the same. "The party" has thus remained for him a special kind of validation. It was destroyed by the Nationalist government but it did demonstrate, for a time, that it was possible to live fully within the terms of South African life. . . .

The second and alternative movement towards an answer was already present before 1948 but became more significant after it. *Towards the Mountain* records in detail Paton's religious upbringing and his commitment as an adult. What the autobiography does not present in full focus is the unusual nature of Paton's religious interests—although I must hasten to add that all I know of his interests is derived from that book and *Apartheid and the Archbishop*. I am not concerned with doctrinal issues and specific forms of commitment on which I would in no way be competent to speak. Rather I am interested in pointing to a consistent element in Paton's thought of religion-as-metaphor. A casual reader of Paton will know that religious reference and imagery permeates his writing but I wish to point to a particular *structure* of metaphor. In *Cry, the Beloved Country* there is a famous metaphorical reference to Eden, "Stand unshod upon it, for the ground is holy, being even as it came from the Creator", and in *Towards the Mountain* this metaphor lies behind the description of the childhood world.

> I cannot describe my early response to the beauty of hill and stream and tree as anything less than an ecstasy. A tree on the horizon, a line of trees, the green blades of the first grass of spring, showing up against the black ashes of the burnt hills, the scarlet of the fire-lilies among the black and the green, the grass birds that whirred up at one's feet, all these things filled me with an emotion beyond describing.

Paton here is mingling almost unconsciously the scenes of his childhood with the pre-lapsarian world of the Garden. The connection is I think highly significant because it unconsciously, but with deep purpose, links Paton's own origins, through metaphor, to a world outside of time and of the fall into history. And in the master concept of the autobiography he sees his life as a progress through the world to another timeless recreated world on Isaiah's mountain:

> They shall not hurt or destroy in all my holy mountain; for the earth shall be full of the knowledge of the Lord, as the waters cover the sea.

. . . Having exposed himself to the devastating realisation of the insecurity and instability of his personal self through the meditation of *Cry, the Beloved Country,* he has in deep unconscious modes drawn upon the resources of the Christian cosmology in order to sustain his sense of identity and purpose.

The Liberal Party was a practical operational attempt to redeem history by bringing the politics of innocence into action. Paton worked at the project with energy and devotion down even to the smallest details of committee work and pamphleteering. His religious assumptions, particularly after the demise of the party, have increasingly become a resource in which the pressure of history and the frailty of the self are subsumed into the larger order of a timeless reality. Both were attempts to meet and answer the troubling questions which he posed at the heart of *Cry, the Beloved Country.*

Forgiveness and Reconciliation in *Cry, the Beloved Country*

Horton Davies

Horton Davies, son of a clergyman, has taught religion at Princeton University. In the following excerpt from his book about how members of the clergy are portrayed by fifteen novelists, Davies discusses the theme in *Cry, the Beloved Country* of the necessity of Christian forgiveness and racial reconciliation. Davies contends that Paton says improvement in education, politics, and social conditions is called for, but Paton also implies that the best hope for easing racial differences is Christian forgiveness.

In the twentieth century the chief problem is the antagonism between Christian principles and race hatreds and prejudices. It is therefore of the utmost relevance that an important novelist, out of the heart of the interracial complexities of South Africa with its many bitter racialists and its few intrepid Christian and humanist anti-segregationists, should have chosen this theme in his moving novel, *Cry, the Beloved Country* (1948).

While the hero is a social reformer who, ironically, is killed by a member of the people he is trying to uplift, he is moved by Christian impulses and convictions. More important for our purpose, however, is that the author, Alan Paton, gives a sympathetic portrayal of two priests, the Rev. Stephen Kumalo, an African rural priest of the Church of the Province of South Africa [the Anglican or Episcopalian Church] and an English missionary priest of the same Communion, Father Vincent. The understanding and compassionate English priest is a portrayal of Father Trevor Huddleston, a great friend of Paton's, who was a notable priest of the Anglican Community of the

Excerpted from Horton Davies, *A Mirror of the Ministry in the Modern Novel.* Copyright © 1959 Oxford University Press, Inc. Reprinted with permission from Oxford University Press, Inc.

Resurrection in Johannesburg. Paton thus seems to be saying that while educational, political, and social amelioration is essential, (and he was himself a teacher and for many years the principal of the Reformatory School for African offenders in Johannesburg), the ultimate reconciliation of racial tensions is to be found in Christian humility, forgiveness, and compassion, which are the gift of Christ, the Reconciler of men with God and with themselves. The constructive meaning of suffering with Christ is 'The Comfort in Desolation,' which is the subtitle of the novel.

MUTUAL FORGIVENESS EASES RACIAL TENSIONS

Reduced to a fleshless skeleton, the story is that of an old African minister's search for his prodigal son, which causes him to leave his little valley church in Natal for the Babylon of Johannesburg, where industrialization, detribalization, and a shoddy imitation of the material aspects of civilization are turning so many of the Africans into prodigals. In the end, after a search that takes him through many aspects of the lives of the city Africans, he finds his son in jail, where he is to be charged with the murder of Jarvis, the social reformer—the two other equally, if not more, guilty accomplices having escaped from justice. The minister also discovers that his own sister has become a prostitute in Johannesburg, the city of Gold, where the African gold miners are not permitted to bring their wives to share their quarters. His brother has become a rabble rouser and critic of the Church in Johannesburg. In Johannesburg old Kumalo is greatly helped by the white priest, with whom he stays (hotels for whites are forbidden to Africans) and who interprets the meaning of suffering constructively. In the end he returns home, saddened but unbroken in faith to find that his great helper is the local white farmer, previously prejudiced in racial matters, whose son Jarvis had been killed by Kumalo's son. Only a profound and mutual and, as Paton believes, supernaturally originating forgiveness could have made this relationship possible. It is in such possibilities of creatively overcoming race tensions that the greatest hope in South Africa lies. It is a novel that avoids the usual dangers of a bitter realism (though it spares nothing in its description of the common decay of European and African moral life) and of a facile sentimentalism (though it shows that Christian love is deeply sacrificial and forgiving in its compassion).

The Rev. Stephen Kumalo is a simple and poorly educated
man. His church is no more than a wood-and-iron construc-
tion; there are no temptations to wealth here. There might be
temptations to prestige and bullying his people. But this humble man is always God's servant, sometimes his bewildered servant, never the master of his flock. He is, of course, in his search
for his lost son, the type of God. In the same way Jarvis, sacrificed though a reconciler, is a shadowy type of God's eternal
Son, Christ. When Kumalo sets out on the search he and his
wife have ten pounds in the savings bank and a little more than
twelve pounds that they have set aside for their son's education.
This money, earned with the sweat of their brows and saved by
much skimping, is immediately used for the great search, for in
their estimation human values always predominate over
money values—and yet to whom does money mean more than
to the honest poor? Yet these savings have to be spent on a journey which—for a simple countryman—is into the anxious fron-
tiers of sophistication and civilization. As the train takes him far-
ther away from the green valleys he loves to the unfamiliar
industrial metropolis, his fear mounts. In Paton's own words:

> And now the fear back again, the fear of the unknown, the
> fear of the great city where boys were killed crossing the
> street, the fear of Gertrude's sickness. Deep down the fear for
> his son. Deep down the fear of a man who lives in a world not
> made for him, whose own world is slipping away, dying, be-
> ing destroyed, beyond any recall.

For reassurance he turned to the pastoral world of the Bible,
which alone was real for him. And even there, in his later
agony and perturbation, he was to lose his way until the Anglican missionary priest helped him stumblingly to find it again.

The old priest's simplicity means that he trusts everyone
and is as easily gulled as his eighteenth-century prototype,

Goldsmith's *Vicar of Wakefield.* In his case it is not green spectacles or a sorry nag that is his undoing, but a fellow African who absconds with his pound note after pretending to buy a bus ticket from the depot. His disillusionment deepens when he learns that his sister, who went to seek her husband, has become a prostitute, and that his brother is no longer a business man but a rabble-rousing politician, symptom and channel of African resentment, who says:

> What God has not done for South Africa, man must do.

The diagnosis of the racial problem is given in several parts of the novel. A younger African priest, Msimangu, who befriended old Kumalo, gives his view first:

> 'My friend, I am a Christian. It is not in my heart to hate a white man. It was a white man who brought my father out of darkness. But you will pardon me if I talk frankly to you. The tragedy is not that things are broken. The tragedy is that they are not mended again. The white man has broken the tribe. And it is my belief—and again I ask you pardon—that it cannot be mended again. But the house that is broken, and the man that falls apart when the house is broken, these are tragic things. That is why children break the law, and old white people are robbed and beaten.' Msimangu continues: 'It suited the white man to break the tribe . . . But it has not suited him to build something in the place of what is broken . . . They are not all so. There are some white men who give their lives to build up what is broken.—But they are not enough. . . They are afraid, that is the truth. It is fear that rules this land.'

The same deep African priest develops his diagnosis more subtly later:

> . . . there is only one thing that has power completely, and that is love. Because when a man loves, he seeks no power, and therefore has power. I see only one hope for our country, and that is when white men and black men, desiring neither power nor money, but desiring only the good of their country, come together to work for it.

Msimangu was grave and silent and then he said somberly,

> I have one great fear in my heart, that one day when they are turned to loving, they will find we are turned to hating.

The liberal and intelligent white man, young Jarvis, had been penning his own diagnosis when death struck him. This was even more subtle, as well as profound, in its exploration of the dilemmas in South Africa and the utter contradictions. Its final words are worth pondering, because almost universal in their scope:

The truth is that our civilization is not Christian; it is a tragic compound of great ideal and fearful practice, of high assurance and desperate anxiety, of loving charity and fearful clutching of possessions.

Meanwhile, as time runs out, Paton hopes that Christians will be able to implement their moral imperatives and by a mutual forgiveness increase the healing of the antagonisms.

PATON PUTS HUDDLESTON—HIS HERO—IN NOVEL

Father Vincent's role is deserving of consideration—especially when it is realized that behind this fictional character stands Father Trevor Huddleston. As Paton portrays Father Vincent, four characteristics predominate. Like all confessors he is an excellent listener, and never a perfunctory one. He knows when a man has become so numb with grief that no words can comfort him. So profound in his capacity for communication that he can speak as the African pastor wishes him to speak, in parables. This conversation is typical of his method:

> —My friend, your anxiety turned to fear, and your fear turned to sorrow. But sorrow is better than fear. For fear impoverishes always, while sorrow may enrich. Kumalo looked at him, with an intensity of gaze that was strange in so humble a man, and hard to encounter.
>
> —I do not know that I am enriched, he said.
>
> —Sorrow is better than fear, said Father Vincent doggedly. Fear is a journey, a terrible journey, but sorrow is an arriving.
>
> —And where have I arrived? asked Kumalo.
>
> —When the storm threatens, a man is afraid for his house, said Father Vincent in that symbolic language that is like the Zulu tongue. But when the house is destroyed, there is something to do. About a storm he can do nothing, but he can rebuild a house.

Father Vincent is also a surgeon of the soul and he now speaks severely, certain that this will best help Kumalo and recall him to his vocation as a priest:

> —We spoke of amendment of life, said the white priest. Of the amendment of your son's life. And because you are a priest, this must matter to you more than all else, more even than your suffering and your wife's suffering.
>
> —That is true. Yet I cannot see how such a life can be amended.

—You cannot doubt that. You are a Christian. There was a thief upon the cross.

Finally, Father Vincent is a practical man and knows that hope arises when a man is reminded of his many tasks and duties and of the dependence of others upon him. He is counseled to pray in a severely practical and concrete way which will also be, though this is not mentioned, a way of healing and forgiveness:

> Do not pray and think about these things now, there will be other times. Pray for Gertrude, and for her child, and for the girl that is to be your son's wife, and for the child that will be your grandchild. Pray for your wife and for all at Ndotsheni. Pray for the women and the children that are bereaved. Pray for the soul of him who was killed. Pray for us at the Mission House, and for those at Ezenzelini, who try to rebuild in a place of destruction. Pray for your own rebuilding. Pray for all white people, those who do justice, and those who would do justice if they were not afraid. And do not fear to pray for your son, and his amendment . . . And give thanks where you can give thanks.

When Kumalo would have thanked the rosy-cheeked priest from England, Father Vincent replied,

> We do what is in us, and why it is in us, that is also a secret. It is Christ in us, crying that men may be succoured and forgiven, even when He Himself is forsaken.

In the novel Father Vincent is merely a profile, taking up only a chapter, but his outline is so firmly etched that the essential priest is here. . . .

NECESSITY FOR RACIAL RECONCILIATION

Much could be written of the poetic quality of the novel and its Biblical simplicity and profundity of speech, of the deliberate inversion of the order of the words to suggest in English the dignity of the Zulu language, of the contrasts between the village and primitive and the city and sophisticated environments, were our concern with the technique of the novel rather than the meaning. Its ultimate meaning is the necessity for reconciliation between the races, which are necessary to each other for the establishment of a harmonious society that will reflect the variety of the gifts of God to men—the example, incentive, and power for compassion and forgiveness that Christ the Reconciler shows and gives. It is only a superficial though obvious and easy judgment that would imply that the white man has all the giving to do and the black

man all the receiving. . . . And while only the antiquarian an-
thropologist (of whom there are few left) and the sentimental segregationist want them to live in their reserves and
their poor city 'locations,' Paton has shown that detribalization has gone too far. They must be integrated in a new Western society in which their human qualities will be needed
even more than at present along with the skills that they
have proved they can learn when the white man gives them
their opportunity.

It is not the least of Paton's distinctions that he has provided a moving sociological document, which is a human
document and at the same time a theological document, a
Christian interpretation of racial tensions and of the spirit by
which they can be overcome. In the same volume he has
also supplied an account of a simple yet dignified Zulu pastor and of a clever but humble English missionary priest.

Christian Affirmation and Redemption in *Cry, the Beloved Country*

Edmund Fuller

Edmund Fuller's works include both fiction and nonfiction, including *Books with Men Behind Them* from which the following excerpt is taken. Fuller contends that although Paton skillfully creates many tragic scenes in *Cry, the Beloved Country*, he also crafts scenes of comfort and love. In doing so, Paton presents a true picture of South Africa in 1948 and at the same time captures the condition of human beings throughout the world.

Cry, the Beloved Country is tragic, but is not a tragedy in the formal literary sense, and it carries the clear affirmation of an element transcending the tragic view of life. This element is Christian. . . .

In *Cry, the Beloved Country* the primary story is pathetic, in that the suffering characters are more bewildered victims than prime movers in their difficulties. The tragic elements are social, and as always, complexly interlocked in cause and effect. The destruction of the soil, the breaking of the tribal system and the home, the tight segregation of South African society producing ghetto slums, the compound system in the mines, the provocative juxtaposition of the haves and the have-nots: these are the specific and local social factors working upon the general and universal human nature. The story is fiction, but Paton says in an Author's Note, "as a social record it is the plain and simple truth.". . .

When any tribal system is shattered by the white man, but the tribal people are not taken into the white man's culture, deterioration and tragedy are inevitable. The African priest Msimangu, in Johannesburg, one of the compelling figures of the book, says,

Excerpted from Edmund Fuller, *Books with Men in Them*. Copyright © 1959, 1961, 1962 Edmund Fuller.

> The tragedy is not that things are broken. The tragedy is that they are not mended again. The white man has broken the tribe. And it is my belief . . . that it cannot be mended again.

Cry, the Beloved Country is a splendid piece of craftsmanship, extraordinary as a first book by a man in middle life, whose work had been in education and penology. The most jaded reviewers were won by the fresh, individual lyricism of its style and the passion of its conviction and its thirst for justice. Paton's use of idioms and rhythms from Zulu, Bantu, Xosa and Afrikaans speech contributed greatly to the fresh effect. Now that his work is well known, and now that other writers have used these language patterns, Paton's style still has its personal stamp, and we must not let familiarity dull our recollection of its first invigorating impact.

PARALLEL CHARACTERS

The book is skillfully constructed in parallels. The simple African Anglican priest, Stephen Kumalo, loses his son, Absalom. The African-English farmer, James Jarvis, loses his son, Arthur. It is Absalom who kills Arthur, for which the state kills Absalom.

By the keenest of the ironies in which the book is rich, Arthur Jarvis was among the greatest friends of the black man, in the forefront of the struggle for justice. The senseless tragedy that links the two sons ultimately links the two fathers. There is no finer scene in a consistently moving book than that in which Stephen Kumalo and James Jarvis first come face to face, by chance, after the shooting, and realize one another's identities.

The ramifications of the story are comprehensive, showing the life of the tribal country and of the city. Through Stephen's journey to Johannesburg to search for his sister and his son, we see how that city, with its mine compounds and shantytown slums, swallows up people and breeds criminals. The quest involves a vivid tour of the native districts, and of the reformatory of which Paton himself had been superintendent. In interpolated meditations on the courts, and upon a new gold field, he deepens the social texture. Most adroit touch of all: the papers and speeches and books of the dead Arthur Jarvis are made the medium of direct polemical statement, and also of growth in the character of James Jarvis.

CHARACTER CHANGE EFFECTED BY LOVE

The father had not approved or understood his son's position on the race question. One could have imagined an implacable hardening on the issue after the tragedy. . . . Instead, the grace that gradually works in James Jarvis is that of love, for he had loved the young man, even without comprehending him. When he is exposed to his son's papers, in the solitude of grief, he finds him for the first time and perceives that to repudiate his son's principles now will be truly to lose him utterly. By honoring and carrying forward his son's actions, something is retained that cannot be lost even in death. It is a measure both of the man, and of the remedial power of love. The new James Jarvis is "a man who put his feet upon a road, and . . . no man would turn him from it."

CONTRASTING CHARACTERS

Among the central threads of the book is the question of Stephen Kumalo's response to his son's guilt, as contrasted to the attitude of his politician-brother, John Kumalo, toward his own son's involvement as an accessory in the shooting.

John Kumalo, whose experience of the city has led him to cast off the faith, is solely concerned with evading punishment for his son and trouble for himself. He is aware that the boy was present, but is successful in obtaining his acquittal through perjury. In John's terms, he has been successful, but we expect that the last state will be worse than the first. The prospects are not bright for his son.

Stephen, on the other hand, faces a profound discovery. Once his son's guilt is established, it is impossible for him, as a Christian, to seek to evade punishment. His most urgent concern is for his son's repentance. He sees that Absalom, whose name, "his father's peace," is as ironic for Kumalo as it had been for King David, is more unhappy that he has been caught than for what he has done. To lead the boy to repentance becomes his first aim. For the Christian, ultimate welfare is not a question of the life or death of the body, but the life or death of the soul.

Repentance is validated by the acceptance of punishment. After the confessed guilt, after the accepted punishment, then mercy (in men's terms) may or may not be forthcoming. . . .

John Kumalo would save his son's life and does not believe in his soul. Stephen would be grateful for his son's life, but would not wish it bartered for his soul. At the end, there is hope for Absalom's repentance—though only God can judge of it.

Gertrude, Stephen's sister, whose degraded state had been the direct cause of Stephen's summons to Johannesburg, is lost. She has gone beyond her personal point of return. The effort of self-examination and rehabilitation is more than she can sustain. She slips away, just before the return of the little party of family survivors to the home village of Ndotsheni.

BEYOND TRAGEDY, COMFORT

Yet there is salvage from the loss and pain. It is this that leads Paton beyond tragedy and that prompts the subtitle of the book: "A Story of Comfort in Desolation." If Absalom has repented, he has not lost both life and soul, as he had been on the way to do. Carried back to Ndotsheni (the account of their arrival is a magnificent lyrical passage), from the certainty of loss in Johannesburg to the possibility of new life, are Gertrude's son, Absalom's wife, and her unborn child. Stephen Kumalo and James Jarvis are enlarged in spirit, and from the spirit come works that promise the renewal of the land around Ndotsheni.

No voice out of South Africa has been so eloquent, so passionately just, with a social morality so deeply grounded in a religious premise. Granted Paton's fine gifts, his work also demonstrates the opportunity offered the writer in a place and time of acute moral and social crisis. . . .

The measure of his books is that while distilling the essence of South Africa, they speak to many aspects of the condition of the whole world. He has struck universal notes, and the world outside his own land honors him for his art, his humanity, and his integrity.

CHAPTER 2

The Novel's Artistic Achievement

Paton's Generosity of Spirit Makes *Cry, the Beloved Country* a Great Work

Orville Prescott

Orville Prescott has served as columnist for *Newsweek*, literary critic for *The New York Times*, editor, and author of many books including *A Father Reads to His Children: An Anthology of Prose and Poetry*. In this selection, he concludes that *Cry, the Beloved Country* is a great book because it celebrates both the joys and sorrows of life with a generosity of spirit, and because Paton expresses a belief in the dignity of humankind.

Any fine novel must be written with sound craftsmanship, must create interesting characters and involve them in a significant situation, must reflect the special personality and point of view of its author. A great novel must do all these things, too, and do them superlatively well. But the extra quality of greatness lies elsewhere.

. . . That extra quality can be imparted by either of two things. The first is a feeling of passionate participation in life, an ability to celebrate life itself as a tremendous experience filled with joy and wonder and excitement, and with sorrow and suffering. Such a feeling springs from a vital concern for human beings, an intense awareness of them and affection for them. This attitude does not depend on any particular dogma, religious or philosophical; but it does depend on a certain largeness of mind and warmth of heart. Great novels are not born in petty minds.

The second factor which can add a quality of greatness to a good novel is more specific—belief in the essential dignity of man, in the capacity of some men to rise to peaks of wis-

Excerpted from Orville Prescott, *In My Opinion: An Inquiry into the Contemporary Novel.* Copyright © 1952 Bobbs-Merrill Company, Inc.

dom, unselfishness, courage and heroism. A novel acquires an added dimension of greatness when its author believes that people can be great. A great novelist in this sense is one who regards the sorry record of human malice and stupidity without evasion, but who recognizes that the vast spectacle of mankind's misery and suffering is shot through with deeds of valor and sacrifice, illuminated by love.

Although the majority of men are afflicted with sadly human failings, the majority are decent (though bewildered), well-intentioned (though ignorant), idealistic (though often led astray). The great truth about mankind is that many men have had visions of nobility and that a few men have striven to attain it. The novelist who shares this vision of nobility sometimes renders his book great by making it a testament to his belief that men and women may rise above their basest instincts, that they may enlist in the armies of righteousness and do battle for the Lord.

CRY, THE BELOVED COUNTRY'S GREAT QUALITIES

. . . Without any of the blind rage which has led so many writers on similar themes into bitterness and dogmatism, without any of the customary oversimplification and exaggerated melodrama, [Alan] Paton [in *Cry, the Beloved Country*] wrote a beautiful and profoundly moving story, a story steeped in sadness and grief but radiant with hope and compassion. He contrived for it a special prose of his own which is both richly poetic and intensely emotional. Anyone who admires creative fiction of a high order, anyone who cares to see how a thesis novel can be written without sacrificing artistic integrity, should not miss this notable book.

Alan Paton is a South African and his novel is about that beautiful and unhappy land. For many years he was the principal of the Diepkloof Reformatory, a Johannesburg institution for delinquent African boys. He has lectured and written on the South African race problem, but this is his first book. He brought to it a rare technical skill as well as the contagion of his love for Africa and her tormented people. He is a man who can see evil and greed and cruelty and tragedy and not sink into despair. He knows that simple human goodness can still be found in a weary world.

Cry, The Beloved Country is the story of the progress of a Christian in whose path many lions stood. The Reverend Stephen Kumalo was an *umfundisi,* or parson, of St. Mark's

Church at Ndotsheni high in the hills of Natal. He was an elderly Zulu, quite unacquainted with the dangers which lay in wait for his people when they left their hungry, eroded country for the great city of Johannesburg on the Witwatersrand. There segregation, poverty, a fantastic housing shortage, temptation and vice destroyed hordes of young men who sought a living in the gold mines. Their tribal society with its ancient laws and customs and moral traditions had been destroyed by the white people. And it had not been replaced by anything else save police and courts and jails.

Kumalo went to Johannesburg to hunt for his sister and his son who had disappeared there. His search was a tragic one. He found his sister first, and she had become a prostitute. He found traces of his son. As he plodded from address to address, finding graver news at each, Kumalo realized that Absalom, his son, had descended into a bottomless pit. So when the good white man who crusaded for native rights was murdered, Kumalo was appalled but not surprised to learn that Absalom was the murderer.

Kumalo's pitiful martyrdom was not all bitterness. His friend, Msimangu, a fellow preacher, proved to be an almost saintly man. The young white man from the reformatory where Absalom had been confined was hot-tempered, but earnest and kind. The white man who was the father of the murdered man was the source of unexpected comfort. The meeting of the two grief-stricken fathers, the proud, silent, conventional Englishman and the humble Zulu, is the high point of *Cry, The Beloved Country.* Then all the complicated social and personal threads of Mr. Paton's story meet and are entwined together in a powerful and extraordinarily touching climax.

Cry, The Beloved Country consists of an amazingly deft fusion of realistic detail and symbolical synthesis of various points of view and emotional reactions. As a picture of the fear and suspicion and hatred which haunt all South Africans, black or white, it is brilliant. The whites, who are so few, are frightened by the blacks, who are so many. Education, public health, social advancements of all kinds are dreaded for their capacity to make the Negroes more insistent in their demands and more conscious of their power. A minority of the disinterested and farsighted whites—and Mr. Paton pays them full tribute—are fighting for social justice. But they themselves are doubtful if they can persuade the whites to love soon enough—before the blacks learn to hate too well.

In conveying his message Mr. Paton never once damages his story, never once mounts a soapbox to orate at the expense of his novel as a work of fiction. His men and women are intensely real and sympathetic persons. Their conversations and their inner monologues are warm with the breath of life, in spite of the cadenced, lyrical quality which distinguishes them. Perhaps people don't really think or talk with such simple nobility of expression; but they never spoke in Shakespearean blank verse either. It is the truth of the spirit that counts, not stenographic reporting.

Fiction [of the 1940s], while often competent, interesting and provocative, rarely discusses an important and controversial subject with both creative artistry and generosity of mind. Because *Cry, The Beloved Country* is both so skillful and so generous it seems to me a great novel.

. . . The nobility in Mr. Paton's novel springs from compassion and generosity of spirit.

Paton Uses Zulu to Convey Positive Values

J.M. Coetzee

J.M. Coetzee has written about the Zulu language and South African literature, and in 1997 published an anthology of South African poetry of the twentieth century. In the following selection, he explains that Paton uses Zulu in *Cry, the Beloved Country* to create a contrast between the innocent, self-sacrificing people of the country and people like the character John Kumalo, who leaves his Zulu village, goes to Johannesburg, and comes to prefer English to his native language.

In Alan Paton's *Cry, the Beloved Country* (1948), the Reverend Stephen Kumalo, whose son is charged with murdering a white man, is told that a prominent advocate will appear for the defence *pro deo*. How can he afford an advocate's fees, Kumalo asks. His friend replies:

—Did you not hear him say he would take the case pro deo? . . . It is Latin, and it means for God. So it will cost you nothing, or at least very little.

—He takes it for God?

—That is what it meant in the old days of faith, though it has lost much of that meaning. But it still means that the case is taken for nothing.

Kumalo's friend is partly right, partly wrong. The words *pro deo* used to mean, and still mean, "for God." In a legal context, however, they mean "without payment." The information about God is interesting historical background, but it carries as little semantic weight as the information that *martial* once contained a reference to Mars. Words do not bear their histories with them as part of their meaning.

Elsewhere in Paton's novel, Kumalo—a country priest on his first visit to Johannesburg—has gold mining explained to him by a fellow-Zulu:

Excerpted from J.M. Coetzee, *White Writing: On the Culture of Letters in South Africa.* Copyright © 1988 Yale University. Reprinted with permission from David Higham Associates.

> We go down and dig it [the ore] out, umfundisi [sir]. And when it is hard to dig, we go away, and the white men blow it out with the fire-sticks. Then . . . we load it on to the trucks, and it goes up in a cage, up a long chimney so long that I cannot say it for you.

. . . The speech of Kumalo's informant here is marked for Zulu origin, not only by the transcription of Zulu words like *umfundisi* but by words like *fire-sticks* (i.e., dynamite), *chimney* (i.e., shaft), and *go away* (i.e., take cover), as well as by an ungrammatical use of the English definite article ("the fire-sticks"). The reader cannot be blamed for concluding that Zulu lacks words for the concepts *dynamite, shaft, take cover,* that the speaker is using the best approximations his language provides, and that Paton has given literal translations of these approximations, in accord with the practice of transfer.

In fact this conclusion is false. The Zulu for mine shaft is *umgodi,* a word quite distinct from *ushimula,* (chimney), whose English origin is clear. The word for dynamite, again of English origin, is *udalimede,* which has nothing to do with fire-sticks. *Banda* (to take cover) is clearly distinguished from *suka* (to go away).

. . . Paton . . . is content to create the *impression* that a transfer from Zulu has taken place. We see the trick most clearly in the phrase "the fire-sticks." Zulu speakers speaking English often have difficulty with the English article, since Zulu has no corresponding lexical form. But it is of course a mistake to conclude that Zulu speakers cannot make the semantic distinctions for which English relies on the article. "The fire-sticks" merely reproduces a common mistake made by Zulus speaking English; it says nothing about Zulus speaking Zulu.

The overt purpose of transfer is to make the reader imagine the words he is reading have a foreign origin behind them. The artificial literalism of passages like the above, however, conveys in addition a certain naiveté, even childishness, which reflects on the quality of mind of its speaker and of Zulu speakers in general.

One of the more poignant conversations in the novel takes place—in Zulu, we are told—between Kumalo and James Jarvis, the father of the man whom Kumalo's son has killed. The two meet by accident. Jarvis, who does not yet know of the tragic connection between them, speaks:

—You are in fear of me, but I do not know what it is. You need not be in fear of me.

—It is true, umnumzana [sir]. You do not know what it is.

—I do not know but I desire to know.

—I doubt if I could tell it, umnumzana.

—You must tell it, umfundisi. Is it heavy?

—It is very heavy, umnumzana. It is the heaviest thing in all my years.

What motive can Paton have for writing *be in fear of* instead of *be afraid of*, *desire* instead of *would like*, *heavy* instead of *serious*? In each case the synonyms translate the same putative Zulu original. In each case the choice is stylistic. The first member of each pair has a touch of archaism; this archaism makes for a certain ceremoniousness in the verbal exchanges, whose effect it is to hold any unseemly display of emotion at bay (the sentimentality of *Cry, the Beloved Country* is largely a matter of ostentatious stoicism of this kind). But the archaism of the English implies something else too: an archaic quality to the Zulu behind it, as if the Zulu language, Zulu culture, the Zulu frame of mind, belonged to a bygone and heroic age.

The Zulu original implied by Paton's English is both unrelievedly simple . . . and formal to the point of stateliness. In its closeness to its historical roots, in its preference for parable over abstraction (Paton explicitly compares it to the "symbolic language" of parable), Zulu—Paton's Zulu—seems to belong to an earlier and more innocent era in human culture. From the fact that Kumalo's politician brother prefers to use English, the reader may further surmise that Zulu is as inhospitable to lies and deception as it is to complexity and abstraction.

The phantom Zulu of *Cry, the Beloved Country* is in fact less the medium through which Paton's characters speak than part of the interpretation Paton wishes us to make of them. It tells us that they belong in an old-fashioned context of direct (i.e., unmediated) personal relations based on respect, obedience, and fidelity. These values are epitomised in an episode towards the end of the book. Jarvis has begun to send a daily gift of milk to the children of Kumalo's village. The man who brings the milk tells Kumalo: "I have worked only a week there [at Jarvis's farm], but the day he says to me, die, I shall die." Self-sacrificial loyalty of this kind won for the Zulus the admiration of Victorian England; it is clearly a virtue Paton approves of. But these words also give us to understand that, by his receptivity to "Zulu" speech and his "Zulu" qualities, Jarvis has crossed the barrier between white and black and taken the place of the chief in his servant's heart.

What, if anything, then, separates Paton from those writers of the 1930s and 1940s who, under one disguise or another, call for the movement of history to come to a halt, for economic, social, and personal relations in the South African countryside to freeze forever in feudal postures? The answer is that, with however much regret, Paton accepts that the economic, and hence the political, basis of feudalism has been eroded by demographic forces. Kumalo's aspiration, in the wake of his son's death, is to hold together the remnants of his community in a muted version of black pastoral. But for how long? The fact is that the exhausted soil can no longer support them. As the young agricultural expert tells him, "We can restore this valley for those who are here, but when the children grow up, there will again be too many." To this young man Paton allots the last and most telling word. To his logic Kumalo and his patron Jarvis, with their fragile hope of preserving an Eden in the valley immune from the attractions of the great city, have no response.

Geographical and Biblical Symbols in *Cry, the Beloved Country*

Sheridan Baker

Sheridan Baker was an English professor at the University of Michigan. His works include essays, reviews, poems, and textbooks. In the following selection, Baker argues that Paton uses geographical features as symbols of such concepts as good, suffering, comfort, and evil.

Paton's moral geography is this: (1) a good valley which has cradled us but which, from social decay and drought, is also the valley of the shadow of death, (2) a beautiful mountain looking down on the valley, sending water and hope, the peak of Omniscience, (3) the city of the plain. The valley is Ndotsheni, the tribal home of the black Reverend Stephen Kumalo. The mountain we may call Carisbrooke, the point at which the reader enters the book to look down on Kumalo's world, the home of the white James Jarvis. The city of the plain is Johannesburg, where black and white pour trouble together:

> Water comes out of a bottle, till the glass is full. Then the lights go out. And when they come on again, lo the bottle is full and upright, and the glass empty. . . . Black and white, it says, black and white, though it is red and green. (p. 17, Modern Standard Authors ed.)

Johannesburg's evil has broken the tribe. There Kumalo's sister sells her whiskey and herself. The green valley of home now runs only red earth when it rains, for energy has shifted to Johannesburg. There black and white collide in violence, which at last miraculously causes water to flow from Carisbrooke down to Ndotsheni.

Because we see mostly through Kumalo's primitive eyes, the symbolism of mountain and valley comes naturally to Paton's book. Kumalo is "a Zulu schooled in English" (15), a Zulu wearing an Anglican collar. The language we are to

Excerpted from Sheridan Baker, "Paton's Beloved Country and the Morality of Geography," *College English*, vol. 19, no. 1, November 1957.

suppose is Zulu takes on the rhythms and phrases of the English Bible, which Kumalo, of course, uses in its Zulu version. An English priest tells a parable "in that symbolic language that is like the Zulu tongue" (108), and we realize that both languages are simple, concrete and figurative, the language of tribes living close to the land. The book's idiom both represents and resolves, as does Kumalo himself, the black-white dilemma:

> ... Now God be thanked that there is a beloved one who can lift up the heart in suffering, that one can play with a child in the face of such misery. Now God be thanked that the name of a hill is such music, that the name of a river can heal. Aye, even the name of a river that runs no more.

> ... But this, the purpose of our lives, the end of all our struggle, is beyond all human wisdom. Oh God, my God, do not Thou forsake me. Yea, though I walk through the valley of the shadow of death, I shall fear no evil, if Thou art with me. ... (62)

The valley of the shadow of death, indeed, is both the valley of Ndotsheni and Kumalo's personal loss of a son, the hope of the primitive tribe where "the dead streams come to life, full of the red blood of the earth" (4). As Kumalo says, only God can save it (233).

JARVIS AS GOD

But God saves Ndotsheni in the person of James Jarvis, who lives on the beautiful mountain and likewise loses a son to the world. We are told that the ground Jarvis farms is holy; its name is High Place. And whether or not Paton intends "Jarvis" to remind us of "Jahveh" or "Jehovah," we soon find him sitting on a stone at the mountaintop, like an Old Testament God, overlooking the world, remote yet troubled by it. Throughout the book Jarvis receives incidental references as God—a letter from him is a "letter from God" (262), his grandson is "a small angel from God" (249), his son is admired "as though he were God Almighty" (139), and so forth. Moreover, his son has gone into the world of Johannesburg; he takes up a mission of mercy; he is killed by the very people he comes to save. And through the father the dead son works a Christian miracle: suffered love makes evil good. Jarvis, even like God, does not really become effective until he learns compassion from the loss of his son.

Through these readings, then, Paton works his magic on the mountain at Carisbrooke. The more clearly we see Jarvis as God, the more we see Carisbrooke's supernatural height. The more Jarvis grows in understanding and goodness, the more we see the mountain as symbol of these qualities. But the figurative Godhead which accumulates behind Jarvis does not overshadow Jarvis the man, and, conversely, ordinary events, under Paton's scriptural spell, take on heavenly illumination without losing substance. Kumalo's Biblical vision—emanating from the beautiful mountain—illustrates Paton's ability to give the modern world an easy traffic with the age of miracles. An automobile, not a chariot, swings low, and the effect is in no way ludicrous:

> While he stood there he saw a motor car coming down the road from Carisbrooke into the valley. It was a sight seldom seen. . . . Then he saw that not far from the church there was a white man sitting still upon a horse. He seemed to be waiting for the car, and with something of a shock he realized that it was Jarvis. (241)

One suspects that black men converted to Christianity by white men picture God as white, Marc Connelly notwithstanding, and that Paton's symbolic use of Jarvis is particularly apt.

Jarvis's personal growth is paralleled by Kumalo's until at the end of the book Kumalo replaces Jarvis on the mountain. Kumalo, too, has a son. In fact, all sons, in Paton's book, bring salvation. The dying valley which runs blood and is resurrected represents the death of both sons, all death, and the life which springs therefrom. The grandson, the nephew, the unborn son, children on their way to school (as if trailing clouds of glory) "coming down from the hills, dropping sometimes out of the very mist" (61)—all bring comfort and hope.

But Kumalo's son brings salvation only at one remove. He kills Jarvis's son, evil making good apparent, black vivifying white. The white son represents the unshakable power of good, transcending death, even increasing; the black son—a kind of Antichrist—represents the hapless innocence of evil in a drifting society. The collision of the two first brings the fathers pain, then mutual sympathy, then some understanding of the good that works in spite of everything. Kumalo's salvation is harder than Jarvis's, and Paton puts his readers closer to Kumalo the Man than to Jarvis the God. Jarvis immediately begins to read his way into the mystery of a good son murdered. But Kumalo has no such comfort. His son is a frightened child, with only a strand of truthfulness left, guilty of mortal sin. Absalom's crime shows Kumalo the hard fact that society may seem the cause but that the individual is responsible. And Kumalo must absorb this bitterness before he can accept the good which flows through the world, even from this tangle. Losing his beloved yet sinning Absalom—a figurative rebel against the righteous father—Kumalo is changed from a kind of primitive tribal leader into the New Testament Father his priesthood indicates.

PLACES AS SYMBOLS

The loss of both sons, the antithesis of both, causes water and milk to flow from High Place down to Ndotsheni, the valley of the shadow, which is, also, this world.

Paton's ancient paradigm of hill and valley as heaven and earth grows clearer as the book progresses. But the more symbolic High Place and Ndotsheni become, the stronger becomes Paton's suggestion that they are Ideals only, remote yet seen, contours to steer by. Only in the evil world is the Son's sacrifice possible and effective. The simple ups and downs of the country are not enough:

> Cry, the beloved country, for the unborn child that is the inheritor of our fear. Let him not love the earth too deeply . . . nor give too much of his heart to a mountain or a valley. For fear will rob him of all if he gives too much. (80)

Arthur Jarvis first learned to love Africa when, as a boy, he rode "over green hills and into the great valleys" (174), but the city on the plain taught him their meaning. It is in evil Johannesburg that Kumalo says, "I have never met such kindness" (125)—"I have known no one as you are" (215). And Kumalo brings his heightened and deepened perception back to the symbolic mountain and valley.

We come to see that the country represents man and the city represents men. The most insistent image in Paton's book is that of a man—first Jarvis, then Kumalo—alone on a mountain brooding over the depths. Carisbrooke and Ndotsheni denominate the human spirit. Johannesburg is a flat turbulence of good and evil which makes distinctions difficult. Johannesburg is a sociological casebook, with stopgap plans and masses of men. The country is man consulting his soul and learning human inadequacy. When Kumalo comes back from Johannesburg with a son lost and notions of rebuilding the tribe, he consults the ineffective chief and the ineffective schoolmaster. He is left with no one but himself, and prayer and God, finally to rebuild the valley and climb the mountain.

The mountain frames the book at either end. From the first sentence we can feel Paton's moral pressure, and we soon notice that it has indeed remolded the South African landscape. A map will show that Paton's beloved country has gently heightened and deepened until it quite contradicts the earth's hard surface. We are surprised to find that Johannesburg, at 5,764 feet, is actually more than a thousand feet higher than our high mountain in Natal, which, though heightened each time Paton returns to it, seemed even at first almost the top of the world. In his opening passage, other mountains seem not higher but merely "beyond and behind"; the great Drakensberg range with peaks over ten thousand feet, behind which lies Johannesburg on its high plateau, is merely a place beyond, with no height at all. We are on a mountain that touches the clouds.

The contradiction between morally-high Carisbrooke and actually-higher Johannesburg works Paton no embarrassment. He can even take brief moral advantage of Johannesburg's altitude, suggesting a civilization and complexity looming over simple life along the Umzimkulu. Kumalo's brother speaks both literally and scornfully of his old home as "down." Indeed, Paton makes the city of the plain momentarily higher than it really is. Approaching Johannesburg, he emphasizes climbing: "Climb up to Hilton . . . ," he writes, "Climb over the Drakensberg, on to the level plains" (15). The level plains seem like the top of a table, reached after much climbing, and so this new country seems to back-country Kumalo, overwhelmed by buildings and buses. But Paton has matched his plain to Kumalo's awe, for, actually, after crossing the Drakensberg at more than eight thousand feet, we drop back down some three thousand feet to Johannesburg, though we do not drop so far as the mountain top from which we started.

Nevertheless, with the mountain at Carisbrooke as reference first for the Beautiful then for the Good, we come to think of Johannesburg as sprawling somewhere on a plain even lower than the home valley. And Paton helps us to this illusion. Leaving Carisbrooke, the train suspends us in unreality. We start in the mist. "The train passes through a world of fancy" (11). Finally, sleep separates primitive heights from the city on the plain.

Furthermore, Johannesburg's relative flatness depresses its actual altitude. On the plain, Kumalo sees "great white dumps of the mines, like hills under the sun" (181). He hears of buildings as high as "the hill that stands so, straight up, behind my father's kraal" (16). He sees wheels high in the air. And when we are in Johannesburg, in spite of one street corner on a hill (47), in spite of walking "up Twist Street" and "down Louis Botha" (44), the mind keeps the city flat. With Kumalo's thoughts we return to hills, and the hills now seem higher, no matter how the land really lies. His return trip repeats unreality and separation (note especially the stagecraft in "rolls away"): "The white flat hills of the mines drop behind, and the country rolls away as far as the eye can see" (219). Again sleep leaves one world behind.

Paton can now afford to wind explicitly down the Drakensberg because from Pietermaritzburg he can carry his readers up and up again, into the heights at Carisbrooke. This trip from Pietermaritzburg to Carisbrooke helps to explain the slightly puzzling road that begins the book: "There is a lovely road that runs from Ixopo into the hills. . . ." Why do we start from Ixopo, never more than a passing reference, why on the road to Carisbrooke rather than at Carisbrooke itself, Paton's essential scene? There is no reason intrinsic to the book, only the reason in Paton himself. He was born in "Pietermaritzburg, the lovely city." Carisbrooke is the point of vision, we infer, toward which Paton climbed as boy and man. It is not his home. It is in the hills beyond, higher, wilder, removed from daily streets, a point to dream from. "All roads lead to Johannesburg," he writes (10, 52)—even the one going into the hills in the opposite direction, for so we assume it was in the growth of this man who began life in Pietermaritzburg, taught school in Ixopo, hiked on up to Carisbrooke, turned around to revolutionize a reformatory in Johannesburg, and poured his experience into his book a generation later. Pietermaritzburg is really the place from which, as we enter the book, we are taking our run into spiritual hills, and Kumalo comes home to the good hills of Paton's own experience.

KUMALO AS GOD

The book ends as it began, at Carisbrooke, though on the peak just above it. From here we first looked down at Ndotsheni and its comic-pathetic little priest, with his dirty collar

and leaky church—grand in the eyes of a child—the rustic
who fears traffic lights and admires a bus driver's courage.
But Kumalo has grown. He himself has even learned amuse-
ment at his friend and at Jarvis and the mystery of goodness
(238). When he climbs to the mountain he is no longer beneath us; the truth of his experience comes to us directly, at
the white reader's own superior altitude. Here, at this new
height, Kumalo replaces Jarvis as God the Father, and the
hill at Carisbrooke, actually lower than Johannesburg, has
now towered up to heaven itself.

Kumalo goes up the mountain to wait for the dawn that
will see his son hanged in Praetoria. We think of Christ going into the wilderness, and of Moses, who talked to God on
mountains: "But even as he started to climb the path that ran
through the great stones, a man on a horse was there, and a
voice said to him, It is you, umfundisi?—It is I umnumzana"(271).

Jarvis goes down the mountain, Kumalo climbs to the top,
sits on a stone, and takes Jarvis's position, "looking out over
the great valley." Here, above the place where Jarvis first
suffered the news of his son's death, Kumalo waits for the
sunrise signaling *his* son's execution for the sins of the
world.

ABSALOM AS CHRISTLIKE

For, though Absalom is a murderer and we see him childish
and frightened, Paton traces suggestions of Christ behind
him nevertheless. Father Vincent, referring to Absalom, says,
"There was a thief upon the cross" (109). We remember that
Christ, too, was executed as a criminal. Absalom is betrayed;
there are three culprits; like Christ naming his successor,
Absalom wishes his son named Peter. On the Mount of Olives,
Christ, like Absalom, prayed his Father not to let him die: "Father, if thou be willing, remove this cup from me: Nevertheless not my will but thine, be done" (Luke 22: 42). Absalom in
prison falls before his father "crouched in the way that some
of the Indians pray" (207). Kumalo, on the mountain, remembers his words, the conventional Zulu responses: "it is as my
father wishes, it is as my father says" (273).

The structure is complete: the two fathers, the two sons,
the two mountains, as it were, at beginning and end. It is the
black Father, with the compassion of the white man's suffering God, to whom Paton leaves the hope of Africa, and its

misgivings, on the highest spiritual mountain imaginable—God in a heaven painful because compassionate, witnessing his son's death and resurrection: "And when he expected it, he rose to his feet and took off his hat and laid it down on the earth, and clasped his hands before him. And while he stood there the sun rose in the east" (277).

The morality Paton writes into his geography, then, is Christian: the salvage of evil through love and suffering. But the geographical pulls are primitive, compelling South Africa's actual geography to match their moral ups and downs. The moral heights of Carisbrooke are Paton's dominant symbol. There we begin and there we end.

Paton's Style Is Crucial to the Novel's Success

Rose Moss

South African–born Rose Moss taught in a girl's high school in Pietermaritzsburg. She has lectured in several universities and is a novelist, playwright, and poet. Moss contends that Paton's liturgical style and clear biblical allusions allow his readers to understand the hopes he and his like-minded countrymen share for South Africa, even though he never names that nation directly.

There is a country its writers do not name. Not all, or not in all works. But time after time . . . we read a circumlocution. Or we read an invented name and geography. . . .

There may be many reasons its writers do not name this country. . . . For some, the name threatens the intimacy of their warmth, because the name means something hateful, but the land is one they love. For some, to use the name would imply political recognition, which they refuse to grant. For some, the country is so doomed one can no longer employ the name it used to have; but the doom is not completed yet, and what will come in place of the doomed name remains unimaginable. They write of people, of birds, of places, but not of the whole under one name.

. . . Alan Paton was the first to use a circumlocution for the place alluded to ambiguously by Karel Schoeman as "the promised land" and by J.M. Coetzee as a "duskland," . . . in Coetzee's masterpiece, *Waiting for the Barbarians,* fused with the United States and other political, historical and spiritual powers and principalities as "the Empire."

Whatever tragic doubts about its identity which this country imposes on its writers, in Paton the circumlocution suited much else in his style: a taste for the general over the particular, the moral over the physical, meaning over sense.

Excerpted from Rose Moss, "Alan Paton: Bringing a Sense of the Sacred," *World Literature Today,* vol. 57, no. 2, Spring 1983. Reprinted with permission from *World Literature Today.*

The lyrical, homesick evocation of one of the fairest valleys of Africa, where the titihoya used to cry, an evocation which moved the world in 1948, comes to our attention as a sacred, biblical place. The lovely road from Ixopo to the hills takes us to a sensuously present Carisbrook, from where you look down; there is grass and bracken about you, you hear the crying of the titihoya. Perhaps one may see the valley of the Umzimkulu below. However, the river's journey from the Drakensberg to the sea and the mountains of Ingeli and East Griqualand behind the visible hills are present only to the mind's eye.

Carisbrook is a liturgical location: "The grass is rich and matted, you cannot see the soil. . . . Stand unshod upon it for the ground is holy, being even as it came from the Creator. . . . Destroy it and man is destroyed." Paton does not care for . . . things that smell so and weigh so and taste so, whose meaning is in themselves. . . . Things do not speak of themselves; they testify to the presence or absence of the Creator.

. . . As a writer, Paton does not intervene to change or repair or prevent the imminent doom his stories portend. He does instruct on how to respond: cry.

The instruction to lament may be as prophetic as Paton's hesitation to name the beloved country. More than twenty years later Coetzee's magistrate uses images of birds and the original untainted garden that echo Paton's to begin an account of how the people of an outpost spent their last year composing their souls as they waited for the barbarians.

> No one who paid a visit to this oasis failed to be struck by the charm of life here. We lived in the time of the seasons, of the harvests, of the migrations of the waterbirds. We lived with nothing between us and the stars. We would have made any concession, had we only known what, to go on living here. This was paradise on earth.

The cadences of mourning are the dominants in contemporary South African literature as more and more writers see and imagine the impasse Paton foresaw in 1948. Given the political hopelessness of peaceful change that would fundamentally reorder the beloved country and allow justice and peace, contemporary writers turn, as Paton did, to individuals. Perhaps in the scope of a single life one may see an image of meaning or decency one dare not look for in the society.

Paton's liturgical style and its clear connections with the Bible and Christian practice offer a way to connect individual virtue with the virtue and sufferings of others, with the history and hopes of devout people in other times and places and, finally, with the story of Christ, whose suffering and death demonstrate that the end of the story is not despair but hope. Most contemporary writers . . . often take a similar stance, perhaps the only stance from which the story can be told. It is the stance of an observer, a chorus, one who knows and feels what happens but cannot prevent it or alter it.

In *Cry, the Beloved Country* (1948) we adopt this stance of liturgical participation as we follow the way of Kumalo's cross, his journey from Ixopo to Johannesburg, his search for his son and the discovery that the youth has lived in what Kumalo calls sin with a woman, the discovery that his son has murdered. As for the son himself, we know him as "son" and "boy" rather than by any name of his own. When the action is not mediated through Kumalo, we learn of what happened through Jarvis. Here too, the actions happen offstage, often in the past.

The movement of the book, then, is not in the actions of central characters but rather in the understanding and feeling of Kumalo and Jarvis. It drives toward resolutions that are symbolically significant. A dam is built. Kumalo waits for a dawn; it is the dawn of his son's execution, but it offers hope of the dawn of another day, the day when justice will light the earth: "But when that dawn will come, of our emancipation, from the fear of bondage and the bondage of fear, why, that is a secret." Paton's fusion of the longing for a day of political and social justice in his country, like numerous other prophetic elements in his early fiction, prefigures many contemporary South African writers who turn to images of a final judgment and a new order in heaven and earth. . . .

PATON'S FAITH GOES BEYOND HISTORY

The split in Paton's imagination between spiritual and physical, which underlies his lack of interest in sensuous qualities and unique characters, shows up in political terms as a belief in a somewhat disembodied spiritual virtue as opposed to material power. Describing the nature and ground of modern-day Christian hope in 1974, he quotes Isaiah and Revelations as inspirations to look to a time of peace that transcends anything we can expect in historical time. The vision of dazzling sweetness, forgiveness and harmony that sustains Paton's hope has little specific, local vindication. He knows that the New Jerusalem, where all tears will be wiped from our eyes, looks like pie in the sky. He makes the claim of faith that it is also pie on earth.

The validity of Paton's vision was affirmed by two early and immense successes. After a life-threatening illness in his early thirties, Paton sought work with young criminals. Thanks to Jan Hofmeyer, then Administrator of Transvaal Province, who was to become Paton's hero and subject of a biography, Paton was appointed to run the Diepkloof reformatory for black boys. Within weeks he had changed the principles of governance from force, rebellion and disorder to respect, trust and internal commitment. One by one he unlocked the gates of the reformatory and left them open. Under the honor system fewer boys escaped for good than under the rule of iron. Versions of the troubling recalcitrant incorrigibles appear in some of Paton's stories and in his play *Sponono* (1965). For the most part, Diepkloof demonstrated the transforming power of faith, care and trust—and did so in a country deeply hostile to Paton's implicit respect and concern for his charges. When the Nationalists came into power in 1948, they rapidly changed the way Diepkloof was run and showed another way to treat lawbreakers and blacks.

Homesick on his first trip abroad, an expedition to learn about prisons and penal reform in Europe and the United States, Paton wrote the novel that brought his country's beauty and sad destiny to the attention of millions. The instant success of *Cry, the Beloved Country*, his first book, brought Paton fame and the financial security to devote his life to writing.

Soon Paton was drawn to realize his vision again in social action as well as in writing. He worked in the Anglican Church with Bishop Clayton, another hero and subject of a biography. When the Nationalists arrested more than 250 people on trumped-up charges of treason, Paton helped establish a fund for the defense and aid of political prisoners. The fund is now outlawed. Paton also became leader of the Liberal Party of South Africa, which advocated universal adult suffrage. The party never sent a member to Parliament and was outlawed by government legislation that prohibited racially mixed political parties. Through speeches and writing at home and (when he was allowed a passport) abroad,

Paton worked to spread the vision of peace through trust that had seemed so efficacious at Diepkloof.

PATON'S STRANGE VIEW OF APARTHEID LEADERS

Paton has never acknowledged that racism and other kinds of evil might be as spiritual as the goodness he presents for us to see, revere and emulate. In a 1982 interview he talked of "the Afrikaner with his strong belief in God, but his real trust in the tank and the gun. As a matter of fact, it has always been." Deliberate, clear, chosen adult malice, Paton seems to believe, does not exist. In his most recent novel he presents a pitiful caricature of evil in a crazed writer of poison-pen letters. When she realizes that she is about to die, she repents. She says of the viciousness she recognizes, "Sometimes it seemed as though the Devil got into me," but we do not believe in the Devil and do not hold her fully responsible.

In history as in fiction, Paton does not imagine that evil can be practiced as an outcome of choice by competent adults who understand fairly clearly what they are doing or whose refusal to understand is itself a choice. Those who seem evil must be mistaken, misled or unfree. In Paton's writing, political monsters of our century seem anemic, hollow men. Paton mourns them in a tone that resembles his lament for Ixopo's lost beauty. Writing of the grand architect of apartheid, Verwoerd, he says. "That there is an element of cruelty in baaskap apartheid and in separate development seems to me incontrovertible." Then he wonders whether Verwoerd knew some of apartheid's implemented cruelties. Could Verwoerd, or anyone, know and relish cruelty?

Verwoerd admired and supported Hitler. He protested the admission of Jews to South Africa in the 1930s. He made Nazi propaganda during the 1940s and was found guilty in a court of law for siding with South Africa's enemy during World War II. He designed the main principles of apartheid . . . and implemented them. He instituted Bantu education to teach blacks that "the green pastures reserved for whites are not for them." During a passive-resistance protest police opened fire, killing more than eighty people and wounding more than 200. Both the scene and the victims' hospital were sealed off from the press and other communication. When an international outcry followed the publication of news and photographs, Verwoerd declared a state of emergency and had thousands arrested between evening and dawn. He appointed as Minister of Prisons and Justice a man who had been interned during the 1940s for supporting Nazi action in South Africa, and he passed laws that permitted arrest without warrant or charge and allowed indefinite confinement in solitary. Some of the arrested went mad. Some suffered accidents: they fell down stairs and died, or they fell from the tenth floor of the police building where political prisoners are questioned. Those events were known to Verwoerd. So were the conditions of life the political prisoners protested: fathers arrested when they came to cities to look for their children, wives who petitioned for permission to visit their husbands for seventy-two hours for "purposes of procreation," black/white wage ratios of one to fourteen. Paton knew what Verwoerd knew. On Verwoerd's death he wrote, "I cannot help reflecting that had Dr Verwoerd been born into a wider world, where his gifts could have been used for the wider benefit of mankind, he might have achieved more than this limited greatness. . . . He could have been great under different stars, but he was born into a society whose definition of greatness is not accepted anywhere else, except in those societies and those minds dedicated to the same ideals of white security, white survival, and, inescapably, white supremacy, by whatever grand name they may be called." Paton recoils from a vision of evil and from a Christianity that accepts Dante's moral ferocity or Blake's observation that "He who loves his enemies betrays his friends, / That, surely, is not what Jesus intends."

Like his hero Jan Hofmeyer, Paton went from a pious childhood to adult life as a Christian without an intervening period of sophomoric skepticism at college to innoculate him with the doubt that marks much twentieth-century thinking. Paton's great move was from his Christadelphian home, through Methodism to the Anglican Church. The great intellectual influences on his life have come predominantly through personal relationships and, until he was in his forties, predominantly with white men. His thinking shows some effects of his distance from intellectual centers. Although the fame of *Cry, the Beloved Country* took Paton's vision to the world, it has not been easy for the world to enter Paton's vision. He mentions Hitler and World War II in biographies, but his imagination seems not to lead him to mention Auschwitz, Dresden or Hiroshima. He mentions a visit by Hofmeyer to India but says nothing of the country. He seems hardly to know of the change from colonial rule that marked so much of Africa and the rest of the world. Speaking to Harvard alumni in 1971, he did not mention Vietnam. He did say that some in South Africa at that time took America's "tribulations" to be "due to your policies of racial integration." Kent State? Watergate? Cambodia? In the same speech Paton approved of American companies that invest in South Africa, because they "improve dramatically the salaries and other benefits of non-white employees." His trust is not in the direct economic effect of these policies, which have affected fewer than $^1/_2$% of South Africa's black workers. His trust is in the "moral pressure" they exert on South African employers "to do the same.". . .

CRITICS CALL PATON'S FAITH OPTIMISM

Paton turns eighty this year [1983], and the world has now heard other writers from his country. What he did not see and would not say are clear. It is clear too that he has disdained the literary objectives of many other distinguished writers of the century. In current South African politics he has little place. In the tides of literary fashion his reputation is ebbing. But what enabled Paton's cry to find resonance in the hearts of millions of readers has not passed. What Paton calls faith, interviewers tend to call optimism. Paton rejects the word. He has never been an optimist. The prophetic imperative he spoke in 1948 remains the imperative. Now other voices have joined his to cry the beloved country.

Paton's images for what he mourns transcend his country. Some of them draw from universal, mythic wells of feeling: the lost paradise of earth, fertile as a garden received straight from the Creator's hand; the birds who sing there; the human life that is destroyed when its precious place is destroyed. What Paton cherishes also draws loyalty: the firmness of people who act from principle and not for show, the strength of those who endure suffering, the sweet dignity of daily acts performed for the sake of another, the goodness of water treated like wine. Paton's remains a voice to hear, a vision to regard.

Cry, the Beloved Country Overcomes Racial Divisions

Sousa Jamba

Sousa Jamba has written for newspapers, including the London *Times*. He has won an award for travel writing and published a nonfiction book, *Patriots*, about civil war in Angola. In this selection, he recounts how Paton won him over from mistakenly thinking that only black Africans could write convincingly about what Africa's black people were experiencing. As Jamba read *Cry, the Beloved Country*, he felt transposed from his own shantytown in Angola to South Africa.

I read Alan Paton's *Cry, the Beloved Country* when I was 15. It was a riveting book. I kept re-reading the words at the beginning of the first chapter. They almost had a magical effect on me. The words described Ixopo, the protagonist's village. I was taken there myself and could see it with my own eyes.

My contemporaries did not think very much of African writers. It was said that they were boring. Who wanted to read about events in an African village? As for South Africa, we all knew that novels from that country would be dealing with apartheid in some way or the other. . . . I shared this view for a while until I discovered that some of the novels in Heinemann's African Writers Series were not boring after all. It was then that I discovered the doyen of African literature, Chinua Achebe—and Alan Paton.

I do remember my copy of *Cry, the Beloved Country*. It was decrepit and smelt of kerosene. Many people, I had concluded, must have stayed up late at night reading one of the best books that have come out of Africa. I never left it behind. I took it to the tavern to drink *chibuki* (maize beer) with my friends and however drunk I would get I would make sure

Excerpted from Sousa Jamba, "Beloved Bookman," *The Spectator*, April 16, 1988. Reproduced from *The Spectator*.

that it was secure. I would get so completely carried away by it that I would forget the pot of beans that my sister had instructed me to tend. More than once, as I scraped the burnt beans from the bottom of the pot, she had threatened to throw the copy down the pit latrine. I later gave her the copy to read. She found it so interesting that she stayed in bed for two days, reading it.

As I began to read *Cry, the Beloved Country*, a strong suspicion began to mount in me. Alan Paton was white and I, like most of my contemporaries, was then very suspicious of white people. We believed that it was all very well to admire and emulate the white man's ways. But at the end of the day we were not the same. White people looked different; talked different; and smelt different. Would they be able to understand black people? I had thought it impossible.

I remember arguing on that basis with an Asian teacher of mine who had written about Africa. (At that time I was writing a story set in Washington, a place I had never been to). We were often told that most of what white explorers such as David Livingstone had written about Africa was false. The time had come for us blacks to write the truth seen through African eyes.

It was at this time that I discovered negritude. My flimsy understanding of it was that Europeans had wiped out an African civilisation that had thriven in the past. I had also dipped into Walter Rodney's *How Europe Underdeveloped Africa.*

I had a bipolarised view of the world. I saw everything in terms of race. White men were there to defend the interests of the white and black men the interests of the blacks.

Why, then, was I going to believe what this white South African, Alan Paton, was going to say about black people? I thought the racial conflict in South Africa was a clear-cut one. On the one hand there were the blacks and on the other the whites. Alan Paton was white, *ergo* anti-black. If he was to treat his black characters with sympathy, then it was mere chicanery, which I then associated with whites.

As I read on, my suspicion waned. I forgot that what I was reading was written by a white man. I was momentarily transposed from the Lusaka shanty town where I lived to South Africa. What I was reading was simply written by an outstanding writer, a genius. He did not pontificate; neither did he reach out for the ready-made clichés as some public figures on our continent are wont to do.

The protagonist, who goes in search of his son in Johannesburg, is not only confronted with the racial problem but with the problem any African who moves from his rural village to an urban centre would face. The violence and the unpredictability of the city would have confounded a Zambian, a Tanzanian or a Nigerian. . . .

I admired Alan Paton's *Cry, The Beloved Country* not because some pundit had uncovered its literary merits. I admired it because it is a great work.

CHAPTER 3

Politics and *Cry, the Beloved Country*

Alan Paton's Influence Extended Beyond Literature

Carol Iannone

Carol Iannone teaches in New York University's Gallatin School of Individualized Study and has had work published in several journals. Iannone argues that *Cry, the Beloved Country*'s political message is more subtle and complex than many of the novel's critics realize. For this reason, Paton's influence extends well beyond the literary sphere.

In an essay written in 1975, Nadine Gordimer declared that South African literature in English had "made a new beginning" with Alan Paton's *Cry, the Beloved Country*, and indeed it could be said that Paton's novel put South Africa on the twentieth-century literary map. Within a few years of its publication in 1948, it had become a worldwide best-seller and was eventually translated into twenty languages. At the time of Paton's death in 1988, it had sold over fifteen million copies and was still selling at the rate of one hundred thousand copies a year. It is not solely in literary terms that a South African novel of the twentieth century must make its mark, however, and Gordimer went on to say that Paton's "was a book of lyrical beauty and power that moved the conscience of the outside world over racialism and, what's more, that of white South Africa as no book had done before."

A 1980 essay was still able to claim that "no single work of South African literature either before or since has attained such fame." Despite Gordimer's own rise to Nobel stature, and the coming to prominence of a number of South African authors, that assessment can be repeated today—no single work has achieved such fame. At the end of the century, it

Excerpted from Carol Iannone, "Alan Paton's Tragic Liberalism," *The American Scholar*, vol. 66, no. 3, Summer 1997. Copyright © 1997 Carol Iannone. Reprinted with permission from *The American Scholar*.

remains South Africa's most significant novel and a rare example of the successful wedding of literature and social conscience. . . .

The novel's success may have been due, in part, to the moment of South African history that it captured, 1946, before the imposition of "grand apartheid" was to consume the country completely in politics. The depression and war had passed. Industrialization and urbanization were breaking down tribal customs, even as the increasing population of blacks and whites in the cities was worsening the tensions under separatism. The novel strips away the surface assurances of white supremacy to reveal what has in some respects become a wasteland—a literal wasteland in the case of the sordid slums and the dying tribal lands, but also a spiritual wasteland, characterized by alienation and mistrust among races and peoples and families and generations. "It is fear that rules this land," says Msimangu, one of the black priests who helps Kumalo.

So painful is the reality depicted in *Cry, the Beloved Country* that when the playwright Maxwell Anderson adapted the novel for the stage (with music by Kurt Weill), he called it *Lost in the Stars,* and made it a cry against a God who had abandoned his creatures. This was done much to Paton's consternation. His perspective is thoroughly Christian, though in the sense of a struggle for the light, not in the application of received truths. The novel manifests both Christian and tragic qualities. The final answers are "secrets" and "mysteries" that reside only with God, and at any given moment the divine may not be evident or clear. The characters must bear up in the face of desolation, injustice, pain, and loss, but there is also hope, comfort, and consolation.

GOOD, LIBERAL INTENTIONS

. . . Avoiding easy answers, Paton enters into the perspective of both "victims" and "oppressors," and demonstrates a humility and acceptance before the unknown and unresolvable. . . .

Paton's rejection of easy racial moralism does not mean that he exonerates the South African system. Far from it. But he doesn't go in for the blanket indictment of South Africa that became typical in later years. Msimangu castigates the white man for giving "too little . . . almost nothing" to the blacks, but be also acknowledges the gift of Christianity and appreciates the good white people who do what they can. On the other side, the fiery speech of John Kumalo demanding higher wages makes a lot of sense, notwithstanding the menacing anger that informs it.

In one of Arthur's writings, a work in progress discovered by his father after his death, Paton provides a lengthy version of his own thought, though skillfully tailored to reflect Arthur's younger, more naïve understanding. Arthur carefully distinguishes what was "permissible" from what was "not permissible" in South Africa's history. Reflecting an earlier understanding of colonialism, he does not feel it necessary to delegitimize all of white South Africa:

> What we did when we came to South Africa was permissible. It was permissible to develop the great resources with the aid of what labour we could find. It was permissible to use unskilled men for unskilled work. But it is not permissible to keep men unskilled for the sake of unskilled work.

> It was permissible when we discovered gold to bring labour to the mines. It was permissible to build compounds and to keep women and children away from the towns. It was permissible as an experiment, in the light of what we knew. But in the light of what we know now, with certain exceptions, it is no longer permissible. It is not permissible for us to go on destroying family life when we know that we are destroying it.

TRIBAL SYSTEM WAS MORAL

This aspect of the novel has perhaps not been fully appreciated. Paton had a tragic grasp of the way good and evil are interwoven in human history. In Arthur Jarvis he created a character who understood the inevitability of civilizational progress and expansion and the conflict and loss that they bring. At the same time, Arthur insists that the colonizers take responsibility for the damage they have done in the process:

> The old tribal system was, for all its violence and savagery, for all its superstition and witchcraft, a moral system. Our natives today produce criminals and prostitutes and drunkards, not because it is their nature to do so, but because their simple system of order and tradition and convention has been destroyed. It was destroyed by the impact of our own civilization. Our civilization has therefore an inescapable duty to set up another system of order and tradition and convention.

Knowing that South Africa prides itself on being a Christian nation, Arthur reproaches it for its hypocrisy, and, by the by, renders a shrewd analysis of the psychology of racism:

The truth is that our Christian civilization is riddled through and through with dilemma. We believe in the brotherhood of man, but we do not want it in South Africa. We believe that God endows men with diverse gifts, and that human life depends for its fullness on their employment and enjoyment, but we are afraid to explore this belief too deeply. . . . We say we withhold education because the black child has not the intelligence to profit by it; we withhold opportunity because black people have no gifts. . . . We shift our ground again when a black man does achieve something remarkable, and feel deep pity for a man who is condemned to the loneliness of being remarkable, and decide that it is a Christian kindness not to let black men become remarkable. Thus even our God becomes a confused and inconsistent creature, giving gifts and denying them employment. . . . The truth is that our civilization is not Christian; it is a tragic compound of great ideal and fearful practice, of high assurance and desperate anxiety, of loving charity and fearful clutching of possessions.

These are nearly the last words that Arthur wrote before his murder.

As bad as social conditions are for blacks, however, they do not entirely explain the senseless murder of a son, husband, and father, and a man "devoted to our people." There were those who had tried to help Absalom. He had spent time in a Diepkloof-like reformatory, where a young official obtained a job for him and arranged for his release so that he might assume responsibility for the girl he had made pregnant. But such aid could not overcome the temptations and confusions Absalom faced in the big city.

At the trial, the judge acknowledges and perhaps even partly concedes the arguments by Absalom's lawyer regarding the "disastrous effect" of tribal breakdown that the victim Arthur Jarvis himself wrote about. But, the judge asserts, "even if it be true that we have, out of fear and selfishness and thoughtlessness, wrought a destruction that we have done little to repair . . . a Judge may not trifle with the Law because the society is defective. . . . Under the law a man is held responsible for his deeds."

Under South African law, a conviction of murder requires that "an intention to kill" be established. Absalom's lawyer argues that the young man did not mean to kill but only fired his gun out of fear. The judge finds an intention by "inference" in Absalom's carrying a loaded gun while breaking into a home. In ruling so, the judge is applying a standard of legal responsibility and conscious deliberation where conditions of social disorder and disadvantage have eroded the moral sense of many young people. "It is as my father says," Absalom dutifully responds to Kumalo's prodding, but he cannot himself explain his own actions. And exactly why Absalom did what he did remains one of the "mysteries" to which there will be no answer.

Nevertheless, Absalom confesses, marries his girl to give the baby a name, and bears up under his fate. His two accomplices, egged on by the militant John, simply deny their involvement. They are completely exonerated owing to what the judge and his assessors deem insufficient proof, while Absalom is condemned to death. Some have taken Paton to be criticizing South African justice, so particular within the courtroom and so negligent without, but the author's accomplishment is that the reader can both understand the reasoning behind the guilty verdict and yet wince at the pronouncement of the sentence.

Ultimately, the humility, honesty, and persevering hope of Kumalo and his friends prove more fruitful than the corrosive anger and cynicism of John and the two thieves (who are involved in other criminal exploits). Good emerges from the wreck of the tragedy. Jarvis and Kumalo meet in a deeply moving but understated scene of shared and interlocking grief. Where Jarvis once saw only "a dirty old parson" from a "dirty old wood-and-iron church," he now sees a human being in anguish as great as his own. Jarvis's eyes open to his son's concerns for the blacks and he begins to help them where he can. He contributes to the boys' club, arranges for an agricultural consultant to help restore the ravaged earth of Ndotsheni, and determines to build a new church for Kumalo. For his part, Kumalo returns home with an expanded family, consisting of Gertrude's little son . . . and his pregnant daughter-in-law. He also becomes more active, working with the agricultural consultant and encouraging the local chief to serve his people rather than indulge his arbitrary and trivial power over them. . . .

After initial widespread adulation, critics began to find fault with *Cry, the Beloved Country,* seeing it as sentimental and propagandistic, more a treatise than a work of art. The novel tends to survive these objections, however, because the whole is greater than the sum of the parts. Wherever one probes a weak spot, the novel resists at some other point; as Lewis Gannett put it, it is "both unabashedly innocent and subtly sophisticated." The mythic narrative involving the search for the lost son blends with a realistic picture of a modern society. The novel's earnest idealism is offset by the amorphous sense of fear that pervades the country and by the suppressed fury the characters carry within them. Kumalo and Msimangu can erupt in anger and yield to subtle cruelty, and the brows of the young official at Diepkloof are constantly knitted against the difficulty of his work. . . .

Dan Jacobson, the self-exiled South African novelist, put *Cry, the Beloved Country* above strictly literary, political, or moral considerations into a category of works he called *"proverbial."*

How to Achieve Justice

Behind much of the criticism of Paton's novel one can make out a political edge. Early objectors to the novel tended to be white South Africans who bridled at its grim portrayal of black life. When the first film version was shown, the wife of the nationalist Afrikaner politician D.F. Malan remarked, "Surely, Mr. Paton, you don't really think things are like that?" The novel was not permitted in the schools until a few years before Paton's death. Later objections came from black militants and their sympathizers, who saw the novel as an expression of white liberalism and mocked Paton's belief in boys' clubs, for example. But the author was not so shallow as to imagine that boys' clubs per se were the ultimate solution to South Africa's dilemma. Paton makes clear in the novel that the renewed ameliorative efforts in the aftermath of the tragedy are a good beginning: but "when that dawn will come, of our emancipation, from the fear of bondage and the bondage of fear, why, that is a secret."

Nevertheless, Paton was modest enough to appreciate the good such measures could do. Paton personally paid for the education of countless black youngsters, gave financial help to many others who were in need, and contributed enormous amounts of time and money to his church, to charitable organizations, and to institutes working for social improvement. These commitments expressed his larger conviction that, as he said elsewhere, "the only power which can resist the power of fear is the power of love"—that the only way to achieve justice in South Africa was through a change in the hearts of enough people to make a difference. The militants who faulted Paton for proposing "love" as a solution to social and political injustice did not seem to realize how much of the groundwork for their political activism had been prepared through voluntary organizations of the kind Paton labored in and supported.

So, too, with the novel itself. Noting the blows it took from later militants, the black South African novelist Richard Rive defended *Cry, the Beloved Country,* calling it a "watershed" in South African fiction in that it brought the racial question into literary purview and widely influenced later writers. . . .

Even disdainful black writers such as the South African poet Dennis Brutus had to admit the novel's power and influence. And while deploring much in the characterizations, Ezekiel Mphahlele, another South African writer, concedes that *Cry, the Beloved Country* is "the first work in the history of South African fiction in which the black man looms so large." Although he did not like the portrait of the humble Zulu priest (preferring the angry John Kumalo instead), Mphahlele implicitly admits that it was true to life.

In Stephen Kumalo, Paton has painted a full picture of an African man, a good but flawed human being, complete with an inner life and a moral compass. The judge's sophisticated legal reasoning in no way surpasses the rural parson's own horrified grasp of his son's murderous act. Furthermore, Paton portrays his black characters in the dignity of individual responsibility even as he shows the restricted circumstances in which they must maneuver. . . .

INJUSTICES OF AFRIKANER NATIONALISM

To the surprise and consternation of many, the 1948 elections saw the defeat of the relatively liberal United Party under the great Boer War general and statesman Jan Smuts and with him his liberal ministers, in favor of the Afrikaner Nationalist Party under D.F. Malan. The Nationalist victory, combined with the success of his novel, convinced Paton to leave Diepkloof, where the new regime would eventually undo all his work. He tried for a while the life of a man of letters. But the worsening political situation in the country and his commitment to service, as well as his relative lack of literary inspiration following his first success, led him to politics.

Like Arthur Jarvis, Paton never condemned the Afrikaner people as such, only the extremes of Afrikaner nationalism. . . . He admired what was good in Afrikanerdom and, unlike most English-speaking South Africans, he knew Afrikaans. He appreciated the Afrikaners' position, their humiliation under the British, and their peculiar vulnerability as an isolated minority culture, even with their numerical superiority over the English. And Paton was always able to see the individual behind the ideology; he recalls in his autobiography that the only person ever to return the salute of the head boy who kept the gate at Diepkloof was an Afrikaner nationalist.

. . . A new phase of Afrikanerdom was beginning under Malan and his minister of native affairs, Hendrik Verwoerd, who was to become prime minister in 1958: apartheid, grand apartheid, total apartheid, "separate development," constituted a social engineering project of dreadful hubristic [arrogant] proportions, aiming to separate all of the races and tribes in every area of life, ostensibly in order to preserve their God-given identities, languages, and cultures, but really to retain white supremacy and Afrikaner security. These were the years when, as Paton wrote, "one draconian [cruel] law after another was passed," backed up by terror and force. . . .

LIBERALISM: HUMANE, TOLERANT, AND JUSTICE-LOVING

In 1953 Paton helped found the Liberal Party to uphold the hope of a non-racial South Africa, and he wrote and spoke extensively on behalf of its principles, both at home and abroad, even after the Party itself was proscribed in 1968. (All reports portray him as an electrifyingly gifted orator.) . . . Paton's politics can make us wonder how "wishy washy liberal" ever became a common epithet. His liberalism was a matter of strength and courage all the way through. . . .

Paton was an idealist, but not a political utopian. He was aware of the built-in limitations in South African society and was patient with incremental change. For this reason he was to fall into disfavor as the racial activism in his country became more fierce, but he stood fast against enormous pressure, mockery, and contempt. . . .

Paton angered the radicals in three areas, writes [biographer Peter F.] Alexander. One, he opposed trade sanctions in the 1980s because he felt that they would hurt the black poor most of all. To this we can add another reason: his experience at Diepkloof, which had taught him that punishment did not lead to true reform; he continued to believe in the need for moral suasion to lead people to free and enlightened choice. He also continued to hold out against violence, although he testified for mercy in the sentencing of Nelson Mandela. Two, he gradually came to favor federalism instead of a unitary state, at least as a transition to one man one vote for South Africa. And, three, he admired Chief Buthelezi, a fellow Christian but, for the militants, a thorn in the side.

Paton took plenty of heat from the government during these years. Although, as the author of *Cry, the Beloved Country,* he was spared arrest and banning, his passport was temporarily revoked, his mail opened, his phones tapped, his house searched, and his property damaged. At certain times he was watched and followed; he received ugly threats and letters from white racists. But his quarrels with the militant left are perhaps of greater interest [in the late 1990s].

Paton demanded to know where the "young white Radicals who sneer at liberals and liberalism" would have been without previous liberal efforts. They "would have been in darkness until now," he asserted. "One cannot measure past labour in terms of present demands." He went on to caution that "if black power meets white power in headlong confrontation, and there are no black liberals around, then God help South Africa. Liberalism is more than politics. It is humanity, tolerance, and love of justice. South Africa has no future without them." Paton's fictional character, Msimangu, says something similar, though more lyrically, in one of the novel's most memorable lines: "I have one great fear in my heart, that one day when they turn to loving they will find we are turned to hating.". . .

PATON'S LASTING ACHIEVEMENT

Although Paton's political labors and political writing pretty much overshadowed his literary work after *Cry, the Beloved Country* . . . it was his supreme and lasting achievement to uphold a model of humanity in the face of suffering and injustice and to have limned it in an extraordinary and enduring novel.

Paton harkens us back to the moral discipline of the early civil rights struggle in [the United States], and he stands for something lost in our post-civil rights era of radicalized demands, grievances, and entitlements: the tragic sense, the mature recognition that "suffering is an inescapable part of life" and that human character is formed in response to it. He held to the belief that love is greater than hate, and that persuasion and reason are better than force and intimidation. He never lost the to us now perhaps distant conviction that "a man who fights for justice must himself be cleansed and purified." He resisted the simplified ideologies of both Left and Right. His liberalism was not the narcissism of good intentions, but the lifelong commitment of a man who saw reality whole.

Cry, the Beloved Country claims our attention through its unembarrassed simplicity, its nuanced complexity, and its textured beauty, as well as through the qualities of mind of an earlier age that it manifests, a turn-of-the-century belief in the dignity of the individual, a modest acceptance of the limits of the human condition, and an affirmation in the power of reason, faith, and goodness. As such it commends itself to the turn-of-another-century's end.

Racial Stereotyping in *Cry, the Beloved Country*

Patrick Colm Hogan

Patrick Colm Hogan teaches literature at the University of Connecticut. In the following selection, he explains that he teaches students to analyze literature by helping them recognize that an author can critique an ideology ambiguously, at once undermining and supporting, criticizing and praising the political system of which the writer is part. Hogan contends that in *Cry, the Beloved Country* Paton criticizes the dominant white racism and ideology that has destroyed the Africans' strong moral tradition, yet at the same time, stays within the dominant ideology by assuming it is the *white* characters who must provide a new, strong sense of order and moral tradition to replace the old one. In this and other ways Paton dehumanizes his black characters, treating them as children and adolescents, inferior to and dependent on whites.

When teaching . . . my aim is twofold: (1) To help students understand the author's criticisms of dominant views, and (2) to help students think critically about positive claims set forth by the author as alternatives to those dominant views. First of all, I distinguish "external" and "internal" forms of critique. By "external," I mean forms that seek to reject the entire social structure in which a given ideology is located. . . . By "internal critique," I mean forms that seek to criticize one part of the dominant ideology by using another part of that same ideology or which criticize actual social practices on the basis of their incoherence with common ideological claims. These can be straightforward representations of hypocrisy that take no stand on the ideological

Excerpted from Patrick Colm Hogan, "Paternalism, Ideology, and Ideological Critique: Teaching *Cry, the Beloved Country*," *College Literature*, vol. 19, nos. 1–3, February–October 1992. Reprinted with permission from *College Literature*.

principles in question, . . . or they can be more politically ambiguous treatments that both undermine and support, criticize and celebrate the system they are representing. Works of this last variety "deconstruct" one dominant position but build up their own views on the same basis. . . .

Alan Paton's *Cry, the Beloved Country* is an excellent example of this final, ambiguous type of critique. As it is a novel of South Africa, the ideological concerns to which Paton addresses himself are centrally concerns about race: the condition of blacks, the relations between the white minority and the black majority, etc. But it is within a largely racist problematic that Paton defines his critique of South African racism. Thus, I preface class discussion of this work with a brief introduction to racist ideology. Students, even graduate students, know of race hatred and prejudice, hiring discrimination, and the like. But most of them—and I include here black American students, nonwhite students from postcolonial countries, and others who suffer the effects of racism—have not considered the ways in which racist thinking is typically structured. Indeed, many of them are only dimly aware that racist beliefs need not involve race hatred, just as many are only dimly aware that sexist beliefs need not involve misogyny [hatred of women].

First of all, racist (and sexist) ideology is always based on an affirmation of difference. Though much recent theory obscures this fact, the first function of ideology justifying oppression is to establish a firm distinction between the oppressor and the oppressed. Nazis did not rationalize the Holocaust by claiming that Aryans and Jews were the same, nor did American slaveholders defend slavery by asserting that blacks and whites share a universal humanity. Fascists, slaveholders, colonialists, patriarchs all seek to justify their domination by reference to deep and abiding differences that radically separate people on the basis of skin color, sex, national or class origin; etc., and that effectively dehumanize members of the oppressed group.

However, not all dehumanization is the same. While there are many variations on this theme, there are three particularly common motifs. . . . I point out that members of an oppressed group are most frequently portrayed as subhuman/ animal, prehuman/juvenile, or posthuman/aged. Each of these types carries with it a cluster of properties defining members of the oppressed group in terms of their sexuality and instinctual life, intellectual capacities, morality, social formations, verbal abilities, stature, color, and miscellaneous physical attributes. In addition, each is typically associated with a range of images and metaphors which are appropriate to the putative [supposed] bestiality, juvenility, or senility of the oppressed group. As it is the juvenile category which is most relevant to *Cry, the Beloved Country*, I will skip the others and outline it briefly.

The juvenile stereotype is first of all the assimilation of members of the oppressed group to children, with the correlate assimilation of the oppressing group to adults. It separates these groups by stage of development, knowledge, maturity—but not, as with the bestial stereotype, by species. There are two common subtypes of the juvenile stereotype: the adolescent and the puerile [childish]. The puerile is asexual or presexual, rowdy perhaps but neither instinct-driven nor moral, playful rather than violent or rational, innocuously anarchic, chattering, small, cute. Members of a puerile group need basic education and the firm, loving guidance of the dominant, "parental" group. This is a common patriarchal characterization of women, and a standard characterization of colonial natives during times of peaceable relations. The adolescent, in contrast, is sexually irresponsible, overpowered by instinct, morally confused, violent, prone to delinquency, rough and deceptive in speech. This shares with the bestial stereotype a characterization of the oppressed group as sexual, violently criminal, and anarchic, but the degree is less in each case and the origin of these tendencies is in upbringing, not biological nature; thus the appropriate response to delinquency is a social equivalent of reform school and severe, rather than affectionate, parenting.

Both of these stereotypes were common in the ideology of "the white man's burden," and they remain common today in liberal views of black South Africans and black Americans. It is important to emphasize that a consistent practice based on such stereotypes can be part of a critique—a specifically liberal critique—of a dominant ideology which views members of the oppressed group as subhuman, rather than merely prehuman. Arguing that whites can and should educate and elevate blacks opposes the idea that blacks are innately inferior, that the appropriate treatment of blacks is punishment rather than (ideologically sound) education, etc. Advocating gallantry towards "ladies" involves, when sincere, active opposition to rape, harassment, and physical abuse. However, at the same time, child stereotypes remain solidly within the problematic which defines and justifies oppression; they reaffirm the superiority of white people and white culture or men and male culture, the absolute necessity of white or male domination—at least until that indefinite point in the future when the childlike blacks and women have matured. Thus they provide an interesting case of ideological critique aimed at the dominant ideology, but nonetheless open to further ideological critique aimed at the underlying problematic. They define, simultaneously, a paternalistic ideology and a paternalistic critique of ideology.

Most of this theoretical material I deliver in lecture to the students, though I do elicit examples and even some stereotype properties from them. Having presented these ideas, however, I encourage the students to analyze the work on their own, with less direct guidance from me. As I cannot adequately reproduce the development of class discussion, I will simply indicate some of the topics I bring up for discussion and some of the points which arise in that context.

CULTURAL SUPERIORITY ASSUMED

The first thing I ask students is very simple: who are the good characters in the novel? After discussion, we find that they are of two sorts: (1) Blacks who have devoted their lives to Christ, and (2) whites who help blacks, prominently including the director of a reformatory for black adolescents. We can see immediately how the latter group functions to critique one form of racist ideology, by holding up benevolent whites as figures to be emulated. This is consistent with Paton's genuine criticism of the common treatment of blacks as animals—of which students can usually give many textual examples. But something else is already implied by the fact that the good black characters are virtually all devout Christians: the cultural superiority of Europe over Africa.

What are some examples of this in the novel? It is easy enough for students to find cases. Father Msimangu explains that he cannot "hate a white man" because "It was a white man who brought my father out of darkness." Another character, told that he has "a love for truth" explains that "It was the white man who taught me." Indeed, the association of Africans with darkness and Europeans with light is ubiquitous in the book. A particularly striking case is at the white-run school for the blind. Speaking of this school, Father Msimangu tells Father Kumalo, "It will lift your spirits to see what the white people are doing for our blind." And later, Father Kumalo thinks, "those who spoke English and those who spoke Afrikaans came together to open the eyes of black men that were blind"—his words having both literal and metaphoric resonance. Even the native languages receive their only genuine value from Christianity, as when Father Kumalo finds "the Zulu tongue . . . lifted and transfigured" through a translation of the Bible.

Thus whites have light, vision, truth, knowledge, and they can guide blacks—help them, educate them. But what of black leaders? Who are the black leaders in the book? First of all, there are the priests. In addition, there are examples of tribal leadership and secular political leadership. Father Kumalo's brother John is the primary instance of a black secular leader. He is corrupt and deceitful, and betrays his brother and nephew at the first opportunity. Moreover, if he were not corrupt, Father Msimangu explains, he would be worse; he would not solve problems, but "plunge this country into bloodshed." The tribal chief, on the other hand, is an ignorant fool, who tries to take over the direction of land development from whites, but quickly shows that he has no knowledge, no understanding, no capacities. Thus black leaders fall into four categories: (1) those who are corrupt, (2) those who provoke senseless violence, (3) those who are incompetent, (4) those who are devout Christians. Moreover, even members of this last group are able to lead only by deferring to whites: by accepting European religion, by rejoicing in the help offered by whites to blacks ("Kumalo's face wore the smile, the strange smile not known in other countries, of a black man when he sees one of his people helped in public by a white man," by standing aside as the whites work out land development plans (unlike the tribal chief), by encouraging ordinary blacks to collaborate with the police (clearly the inverse of inciting bloody revolution), etc. Indeed, the narrator and the black characters are quite explicit in granting only whites adequate intelligence for leadership. For example, Kumalo is good and sympathetic, but painfully simple. And Father Msimangu speaks of four leaders, one European, one of mixed European and African descent, and two African: "Professor Hoernle . . . he was the great fighter for us . . . he had Tomlinson's brains, and your brother's voice, and Dubula's heart, all in one man." Africans may have deep feelings, or deep voices, but only the Europeans and those with European blood have "brains." (Though ultimately of the same general category as Kumalo—a black man filled with Christian love, who can act for the good if led by whites—Dubula is a secular activist and thus a partial exception to the preceding schema. He is worth discussing in class, but I leave him aside here due to constraints of space.)

THE NOVEL'S PATERNALISM

And what of ordinary blacks in this book—what are they like? They are murderers, thieves, bootleggers, and prostitutes. And the novel repeatedly tells us that these crimes—not the casual brutalization of black men and women, not the denial of political and economic rights to the overwhelming majority of the population—are the big problems in South Africa; they are, after all, the problems of Kumalo's own family, and, more importantly, they are crimes which affect whites. The narrator informs us about one region where "most of the assaults reported were by natives against Europeans." As Father Msimangu laments, today "children break the law, and old *white* people are robbed and beaten" (emphasis added), and as Father Kumalo reflects, on the edge of despair, "His son had gone astray. . . . But that he should kill a man, a *white* man!" (emphasis added). And what is the cause of these problems? Again, it is not political oppression and economic exploitation. Rather it is the lack of an adequate familial structure in which a strong moral tradition can be handed down—and specifically the failure of Europeans to provide such a system, their failure to accept parental responsibilities.

The clearest statement of this paternalism is in the fragment of a treatise left behind by Arthur Jarvis, the absent hero of the novel, the great fighter for blacks who was killed by black criminals, a man directly associated with two other murdered liberators, Abraham Lincoln and Jesus Christ. Here, I ask my students to analyze the excerpt of Jarvis' writing in detail, for in this passage the novel's paternalism is fully explicit. Jarvis insists that the destruction of native culture was "permissible" because of that culture's "violence and savagery . . . its superstition and witchcraft." But because of this destruction, "Our natives today produce criminals and prostitutes and drunkards." He continues, "Our civilization has therefore an inescapable duty to set up another system of order and tradition and convention." In this context, students typically discuss the implicit characterization of the native peoples as "our" children—puerile or adolescent—whom "we" (i.e., whites) have the right and duty to educate and reform. In addition, we discuss other presuppositions of the fragment, for example that contained in Jarvis' reference to South African resources as "our great resources," where the "our" clearly refers to Europeans.

Depending on the class, we might conclude by discussing the reception of the novel. Why would *The New Republic* refer to this as "one of the best novels of our time," and why would it be such a bestseller, a novel still required reading in some American high schools? Ideally, I would eventually lead this into a discussion of the function of liberalism and paternalism, not only in South Africa, but in the United States as well, where the debate over minorities tends to be defined within quite comparable parameters [limits]. Even when we find the ideological complicity of Paton's paternalistic critique—its strict adherence to a racist problematic—quite obvious, many of us may still fail to recognize a similar complicity in writings on race by prominent white American liberals. While it is valuable to help students understand the operation and critique of dominant ideology in any context, it is most valuable when they can apply and extend that understanding within the context of their own society.

Teaching *Cry, the Beloved Country* in the Classroom

Robert Mossman

A teacher at St. Gregory School in Tucson, Arizona, Robert Mossman contends that because South African society is so thoroughly polarized, no one work of literature can capture the entirety of what it means to be South African. Acknowledging that *Cry, the Beloved Country* is the most frequently taught South African novel, he strongly recommends that a second novel, by an author from a different racial group, be studied.

The literature of South Africa provides a unique microcosm for examining issues of race, class, and gender. . . .

A study of South African literature [by] American students can also be instructive about the difficulties and problems of reading literature from a divided society.

One of the enduring and saddest legacies of the apartheid system may be that no one—White, Black, Coloured (meaning of mixed-race in South Africa), or Asian—can ever speak as a "South African." Because of the extreme polarization on racial lines, writers can speak only from their own perspective as a White, Black, Coloured, or Asian. This is a heavy burden. No one will ever write the definitive "South African" novel.

Nonetheless, with the exception of Nigeria, South Africa has one of the richest and certainly most extensive literatures in sub-Saharan Africa. It arises from the oral traditions of Zulus, Xhosa, Pedi, Venda, Tswana, Sotho, and Swazi. It has created a new language, Afrikaans, developed by the descendants of the Dutch. And it has always been dominated by English and its many and varied traditions. Indeed, En-

Excerpted from Robert Mossman, "South African Literature: A Global Lesson in One Country," *English Journal*, vol. 78, no. 8, December 1990. Reprinted with permission from the National Council of Teachers of English.

glish is now the preeminent language of most literature written in South Africa. The famous 1976 Soweto uprising was initiated by Black high-school students who wanted to maintain English as the language of instruction rather than Afrikaans, which the government preferred.

A study of South African literature in an American classroom, to be valid and legitimate, cannot consist of merely one work and be successful. By the very fact of the polarized nature of the apartheid system and the literary responses to it, students must encounter and examine works which represent viewpoints from different racial perspectives. . . .

The most frequently taught work of South African literature in American classrooms is *Cry, the Beloved Country* by Alan Paton. The limitations of this novel illustrate the problems associated with teaching only one work of South African literature. . . .

Paton's tone is preachy and positive. Despite the horrific evils he alludes to, Paton is the didactic preacher. He wants us to believe that things will get better if only the young, symbolized by the two youngsters who appear near the end of the book, can communicate and thus understand each other.

. . . Paton's view of South Africa in retrospect seems at best overly optimistic; at worst, simplistic and patronizing.

The issue of Whites patronizing Blacks is crucial in South African literature. Is it possible for a White writer, no matter how sympathetic to the Black cause, to understand and realistically represent the status and the stories of South Africa's Blacks, Coloured, or Asians? This issue can be explored in the classroom and expanded to obviously similar problems around the world and more particularly here in the United States.

How can the "first" world speak to or for the "third" world? How can it presume or prescribe answers without intense scrutiny of both its motivations and its objectives? Can writers speak cogently from outside their own social, economic, religious, ethnic, or racial heritage? Certainly, many do! How do we as readers and teachers of readers make them and ourselves aware of how, when, and why this is done?

If *Cry, the Beloved Country* must be taught in the curriculum, then it should be taught in conjunction with *Mine Boy* by Peter Abrahams (1975). Like Absalom Kumalo in *Cry, the*

Beloved Country, Xuma, the hero of *Mine Boy,* arrives in the big city from a rural area to work. But his story is told from the perspective of the township. We feel, hear, smell, and experience the life of the South African township in all of its intimate detail. Instead of Paton's sophomoric poetry, we hear the cadence of dance and song and authentic township language. Read together, these two novels offer a compelling comparison of how writers create, what language they use, what biases they have, and how these are conditioned by their color.

South Africa offers many other pairs of books which can be studied successfully in conjunction:

1. Athol Fugard's *Tsotsi* (1983) and Alex La Guma's *Walk in the Night* (1968) offer portraits, one White, one Coloured, of young men and their grim fights for survival in the gritty townships.

2. Breyten Breytenbach's *True Confessions of an Albino Terrorist* (1986) and Alex La Guma's *Stone Country* (1974) are prison narratives detailing and documenting the horror of life in prison under the Nationalist government.

3. Nadine Gordimer's *Burger's Daughter* (1980) and Andre Brink's *Dry White Season* (1984) offer two perspectives, one female and one male, of how Whites try to come to grips with what it means to be White and privileged in South Africa.

4. Richard Rive's *Buckingham Palace, District Six* (1986) and Andre Brink's *Rumours of Rain* (1984) offer wonderfully vivid and detailed portraits of communities: the Cape Coloureds of District Six in Capetown and the Afrikaaners of Transvaal cities and rural farms.

5. Nadine Gordimer's *July People* (1982) and J.M. Coetzee's *Life & Times of Michael K* (1985) suggest visions from a heroine and hero of what life may be like in South Africa after a successful Black revolution.

6. Sipho Sepamla's *Ride on the Whirlwind* (1984) and Mongane Serote's *To Every Birth Its Blood* (1983) provide strikingly personal and intense accounts of life in the townships, Soweto and Alexandra, during the uprisings of the late 1970s.

. . . There are many other fine South African writers. A study whether of only two works in conjunction or of many works will provide an exciting stimulus. It will offer to American students a searingly real world which is amazingly similar to their own experiences.

Cry, the Beloved Country Is Visionary but Honest

F. Charles Rooney

In the following selection, theologian F. Charles Rooney argues that Paton is not a mere craftsman or a propagandist, but an artist telling a realistic story of power, compassion, insight, and significance.

Depending on one's point of view, the distinguishing mark of literature is to give pleasure, or to appeal to the emotions, or to uplift the reader; and so on. Yet no serious reader will accept these statements as encouraging or even permitting propaganda, be it religious, social, political or economic. Certainly some very good literature can have elements of propaganda; but whatever propaganda there is weakens the work and detracts from it.

It is interesting, yet not altogether surprising, that one of the most skilled and sensitive writers [in 1961], Alan Paton, has been suspected of moralizing. Everything about him seems to lend basis to this suspicion. He is an ardent and inspired advocate of racial justice in the most professedly segregationist nation in the world, the Union of South Africa. He is a former reformatory warden and has pioneered for institutional reform in a land not reputed to be especially progressive. And finally (worst of all!) he has written three books, each of which is built upon the foundations of his personal experience. His first two, *Cry, the Beloved Country* and *Too Late the Phalarope* unhesitatingly grapple with striking, race-conflict themes.

The third, *Tales from a Troubled Land*, a book of short stories focuses predominantly on situations in a boys' reformatory. With such an obvious parallel between his life and writing, Paton's readers almost automatically assume that

Excerpted from F. Charles Rooney, "The 'Message' of Alan Paton," *The Catholic World*, vol. 94, no. 160, November 1961.

he has a message to put across in his books. And how, one asks, can such a message be anything but propaganda?

With so many counts against him, a writer would have to be especially talented and restrained to keep himself sufficiently out of his stories—to keep his aesthetic distance. Only a highly disciplined writer could keep from haranguing. Yet Paton's readers know that he accomplished exactly that. He tells two taut absorbing stories with characters unmatched in contemporary fiction for their spontaneity and inherent drama for being themselves.

Thus the onlooker is hard put to account for the charge against Paton of propagandizing . . . unless he attributes to the critic either an indiscriminating biocritical method or insufficient objectivity. To bring an author's personal life into the evaluation of his work is fraught with the danger of unjustified assumption. This peril is nowhere more evident than in the criticism of Paton's two novels. A more accurate index of his accomplishment is the warm acceptance of his tender, yet powerful, stories by thousands of perceptive readers. However, the publisher's eulogies of Paton as a humanitarian only bolster suspicions of "preaching."

The most severe effect of this prejudice about his "purpose" is that it puts a shadow on his stature as a writer. Alan Paton is no mere craftsman though his diction and rhythm are stirring. He is a mature artist telling a story of power, insight and significance. He searches the dilemma of man's fear and disregard of his fellows with all the compassion and force of Steinbeck in *Grapes of Wrath*. Yet he has what Steinbeck never had, a vision of the life of the spirit. He has all Steinbeck's heart, plus *soul.*

For Paton love, supernatural forgiving love, is the imperative of life; without it life is destroyed. It is the vacuum created by fear and hate that is the cause of all conflict in his novels; his insight into this void has set Paton's novels not only beyond but on a different plane from the bulk of modern fiction.

Cry, the Beloved Country is a great novel, but not because it speaks out against racial intolerance and its bitter effects. Rather the haunting milieu of a civilization choking out its own vitality is evoked naturally and summons our compassion. There are no brutal invectives [insults], no blatant injustices to sear the reader's conscience, no vicious hatred, no righteously unleashed passion. It is a great compliment to Paton's genius that he communicates both a story and a lasting impression without bristling, bitter anger.

Restraining himself and the reader within the bonds of probability, he etches the portrait of the family of Stephen Kumalo, a humble colored Anglican parson. The family is separated and destroyed by the advent of an industrial culture in South Africa. Kumalo's son, Absalom, and Arthur Jarvis, the white man whom the son has accidentally killed, are both destroyed by the fear and distrust that have accompanied technological "progress."

PATON DOES NOT ACCUSE

But this is a silent destruction, one for which the blame is not pinned down; the directions of real life are not so apparent. The reader's impression of the milieu Paton describes is rather of *corrosion*. Paton's protest to injustice consists in pointing out, not accusing. The South Africa we find in his books is a manifestation of Christian heart that has forgotten what it should be. It has seen itself and has found no love that might embrace all. Therefore it proceeds to exclude, to segregate, to separate, to fear. Self-enclosed, the soul of a nation quickly begins to distort everything it sees until finally it finds that life itself has been squeezed of every value that makes it worthwhile and noble. Indeed the total impression one gets from Paton's work is of a nation frightened by its own shadow. This is the tragedy that elicits our compassion.

> Cry, the beloved country, for the unborn child that is the inheritor of our fear. Let him not love the earth too deeply. Let him not laugh too gladly when the water runs through his fingers, nor stand too silent when the setting sun makes red the veld with fire. Let him not be too moved when the birds of his land are singing, nor give too much of his heart to a mountain or a valley. For fear will rob him of all if he gives too much.

These are words of a people, forcing themselves up from the wellsprings of the human spirit. They are the warning cries of a lover fearing for the beloved. Here, as throughout the novel, there is no maudlin commentary from the author. Rather the innermost emotions of a whole nation are expressed in various ways, in many passages scattered throughout the book to emphasize their independence of any particular figure in the story.

AN EXAMPLE OF PATON'S TECHNIQUE

A seeming interpolation by the author (as narrator) in chapter twenty-eight provides an excellent example of Paton's technique. The passage is a stinging rebuke to the gold fever of the rich white men who own the mines and unmercifully exploit native labor. It concludes with a mention of the plan of Sir Ernest Oppenheimer, a farsighted white leader, to permit native mine workers to live in villages with their families instead of in compounds:

> They want to hear your voice again, Sir Ernest Oppenheimer. Some of them applaud you, and some of them thank God for you in their hearts, even at their bedsides. For mines are for men, not for money. And money is not something to go mad about and throw your hat into the air for. Money is for food and clothes and comfort, and a visit to the pictures. Money is to make happy the lives of children. Money is for security, and for dreams, and for hopes, and for purposes. Money is for buying the fruits of the earth, of the land where you were born. . . . No second Johannesburg is needed upon the earth. One is enough.

It is not hard to imagine a socially conscious writer stepping beyond the legitimate limits of the novel form to express such sentiments. But Paton does not do this. Chapter twenty-eight is a natural and integral part of his story, a sequel to the brilliant ninth chapter which describes the overnight rise of a shanty village. To deny the kind of judgment expressed in the above passage a legitimate place in literature is surely to take such an exclusive and rarified view of the writing art that it no longer touches life.

Another startling reflection on the inner corruption of South Africa might seem, at first, open to criticism as extraneous to the story, put in simply to make a point.

> In the deserted harbour there is yet water that laps against the quays. In the dark and silent forest there is a leaf that falls. Behind the polished panelling the white ant eats away the wood. Nothing is ever quiet, except for fools.

Yet here too we are eventually forced to admit Paton's genius to express his nation's pulse and his people's conscience. Here we see not a lone angry commentator but a compassionate sufferer witnessing the decline of that which he loves. We do not hear the clear voice of the author telling us what to think; these "asides" always spring from the story: In fact we might wonder at the reticence if they were unsaid, for the very rocks cry out. . . .

JUDGING THE WRITER'S VISION

We may point out three significant criteria for judging whether a writer has shared a vision of reality with us or has only told us something. The first is whether the story conforms to the demands of reality or the plot is labored and the characters stereotyped. Paton satisfies this requirement admirably. His Christianity and talent have conspired to produce a just picture of the relationship of the races. Real guilt is punished (Absalom for murder) . . . it is the *spirit* and *degree* of punishment—not its injustice—that Paton upbraids.

He admits virtue and good will among those who, almost inculpably [without blame], demand such unchristian laws, although his equity does not prevent him from being slightly cynical at times about that virtue. . . . These are men who have lost their identity in the faceless group, like the lynching party in *To Kill a Mockingbird.* If the fickleness of human justice is reproved, still no barbs are hurled. It is difficult to envisage a more fair and dispassionate characterization of the conflict he presents. And because of the writer's fidelity to fact the story rings true.

The second rule of judgment is that the writer must not be expressing merely personal prejudices or his favorite "cause." Every sentiment must be not his own private feeling but the expression of a widely felt or universal feeling or conviction. [The] novel presents [a] plot that commands our assent by the inner cogency of [its] appeal to the reader's sense of justice and his compassion. There is nothing petty, nothing that the reader feels is being imposed upon him.

The third standard, closely related to the second, is that every reflection upon moral or ethical issues should find expression naturally within the framework of the story. This criterion is more a technical problem than the other two, but it can only be satisfied by a valid artistic intuition. That is, the writer cannot choose to expound some didactic [moral] instruction, and then decide who will say it. What is said must grow out of a fully developed, real character who can lay claim to our acceptance as a genuine person who *should* say this. As has been pointed out in several characteristic instances, Paton has not succumbed to the temptation of simply saying something. In his novels the story is the thing, and whatever is said must grow out of the story.

Cry, the Beloved Country Is Unrealistic

A.A. Monye

> A lecturer at the University of Benin, Nigeria, A.A. Monye contends that Paton's characters in *Cry, the Beloved Country* are flat and dismisses as simplistic and unrealistic Paton's belief that love rather than violence would solve the problems of colonial brutality and oppression of blacks in racist South Africa.

Alan Paton must have been influenced by the historical trends in South Africa by the time he wrote *Cry, The Beloved Country*. There is therefore need to understand the history behind this novel. At the time it was published, barely three years after the Second World War, *Cry, The Beloved Country* helped to influence South African writing, particularly with regard to such issues like the oppression of the Black South Africans before, during and after these years of global unrest. The novel was received with wide acclaim as Black Americans received *Uncle Tom's Cabin*. Like the latter novel, it held hope for the oppressed blacks in Apartheid South Africa in that it helped to focus world attention on the lot of these victims of racism just as *Uncle Tom's Cabin* did so much to expose the living conditions of Black Americans. . . .

Although Alan Paton's *Cry* draws our attention to and sympathy for the oppressed Black South Africans, the emotions it compels on us do not offer any positive solution to the problems of racism and colonial brutality in South Africa. We are merely invited to cry for a bruised and bleeding land and people. But the question is: Should we merely Cry? Is crying all we can do for these unfortunate victims of apartheid?

THE BROTHERLY LOVE SERMON

Again, in his message, Alan Paton seems to be preaching the Biblical sermon of brotherly love, like the one which Rev.

Excerpted from A.A. Moyne, "*Cry, the Beloved Country*; Should We Merely Cry?" *Nigeria Magazine*, vol. 144, 1983.

Stephen Kumalo and Mr. Jarvis very much belatedly strain in vain to forge. It should be noted that this love was incidental. The two old men stumbled into it through their sons, Absalom and Arthur Jarvis. It was after the former had inadvertently killed the latter that the two fathers, linked by this sad incident, came to know how near and yet distant to each other they had been all the years.

This sermon—'love thy neighbour as thyself', is meaningless in a society where the basic requirements of life are denied a section of it. It is useless in a system where a negligible number of the population arrogate to [claim for] themselves certain privileges and rights which they deny an integral part of that same just because of the pigmentation of the skin. To preach love to a people who are denied all their human rights, a people, who denied their ancestral heritage, are forced to the shanties and ghettoes by aliens who now occupy the richer parts of their land, is quite unrealistic.

REV. KUMALO, THE SACRIFICIAL LAMB

Love in this society will only be realistic when what has been denied the Black South African is restored to him. But since the enemy is not prepared to do this the only alternative left to the oppressed is to greet the situation with violence in order to regain his lost ancestral heritage. He has to go to the city to do the battle with the enemy. It is on this note that we see the journey made by the oppressed blacks to the big city of Johannesburg as symbolic. It is symbolic in that it is a journey which every oppressed black in South Africa has to undertake in order to realise himself. It is however pathetic that Johannesburg symbolises destruction, for as the inferno which destroys everything that comes near it, so does it destroy the black man. Yet, it is imperative that this journey should be made because it is through it that the oppressed black will have the opportunity to confront his oppressor.

Yet, in his naivety, Rev. Kumalo is opposed to the idea of making this all-important journey to the city where the native will do battle with the white usurpers. It is partly because of his lack of a thorough understanding of the significance of this journey that the old reverend is sad when his sister Gertrude, who had gone in search of her husband, would not return to the village, Ndotsheni. That is why Rev. Kumalo complains that youths have deserted the village and gone to the city. That too is why he is shocked that his brother, John Kumalo, who understands the system more than he does, would not heed his advice that they should return to Ndotsheni but instead chooses to remain in the city where he would fight it out with the white enemy. We should remember that Rev. Kumalo's journey to the city was motivated by the letter from Theophilus Msimangu, a man he had never met in his life. In the letter Rev. Kumalo is asked to come and save a mother and a son lost in the labyrinth of the South African predicament. Rev. Kumalo is now prepared to discharge this priestly duty. Ironically however, he does not know that his own son Absalom needs salvation more than the people he now feels he has to go and save as a priest of God. Surprisingly enough, in spite of his agony in the city, in spite of the revelation made to him that there is need for him to lead his oppressed people in the fight against an oppressive system that has sentenced his son to death, a system that does not concern itself with the

PATON'S CHARACTERIZATION IS FLAWED

David Rubidari accuses Alan Paton of creating insignificant, flat black characters in Cry, the Beloved Country. *Rubidari calls Stephen Kumalo undeveloped as a character, and along with Msimangu, naïve and sentimentalized.*

[*Cry, the Beloved Country*] is in many ways unique for being the first work in the history of South Africa in which a black man is the main character; and yet what do we have in this novel? A story in which the characters, that is the people who really matter, are of secondary importance. They all seem to be pathetically flat; as we read on we are saddled with the load of the author's monumental sermon on 'Comfort in desolation' . . . 'So in my suffering I can believe', is all that Rev Stephen Kumalo seems to say throughout much of the book. Mr Paton's commentator Msimangu remains untouched by the events in the story. Both characters are cloaked in a Christlike atmosphere, and they behave with a naïveté of children. They hardly develop. They are always trembling with humility and accepting the scheme of things as a matter of course. Even after his bitter experience in the city, Kumalo can still address the white boy from Jarvis' farm as "Inkosana" (Little master). This has been the general trend of most white writers in Africa today, a pattern that begins with an evangelical missionary zeal in the white man's image of the non-white and is justified by an assumption that they welfare of his people, Rev. Kumalo would not act. He can only lament the imminent death of his son.

Ezekiel Mphahlele condemns Rev. Kumalo for his cowardice when of him he writes:

> Kumalo remains the same suffering, Christlike, childlike character from beginning to end. He is always trembling with humility. He accepts the scheme of things: 'No, nothing, only more fear and more pain. There is nothing in the world but fear and pain!' [Kumalo fails to remember that there is need for action.] He is always bewildered. Even after his bitter experiences in the city, he can still address the white boy, 'when you go, something bright will go out of Ndotsheni'. The priest can still end his letter of condolence to Jarvis, 'Your faithful servant.' Kumalo represents the African of the old generation who behave ordinarily in the presence of their fellow-Africans but with self-effacement in the presence of the white people; the long-suffering type that gets all the kicks and wishes to give none; the type that give a stock response to violent situations, bear and suffer.

know the answers not only for themselves but also for the poor natives. They need to justify not only themselves but also the black man; the Kumalo type role is highly sentimental—and one most attractive to the white novelist with a liberal tarnish. In the midst of so much pain, fear and dishonesty, he seems to say *here* is a black man who does not hate you, who harbours no bitterness. And he is a black man, too, one of the race that is often despised. Have you no reverence for such dignity? And so on. Sophiatown, the slum of flick knives, violence, debauchery, dissipation, of violent jazz and *kwela*, leaves Mrs Lithebe an almost angelic figure. She is untouched by it; she fits into this sermon and must not get out of hand. The tremendous forces and complications that face the boy Absalom and his mistress do not seem to really matter to the total complex of this violent situation. We are hardly allowed to see Absalom's demoralization growing. We do not even know what he thinks about himself and the social order in which he has been clamped as in a vice. When we come face to face with him, he is a frightened young man being sacrificed, waiting in jail for the hangman the next morning, as in the biblical image of the sacrifice of the young Isaac by Abraham. The image, the message, the sentiment that matters, the conflict that must bring violent power to the final totality are hardly exploited by the writer. The characters in themselves, as people, do not seem to count for much.

G.D. Killam, ed., *African Writers on African Writing*, 1973.

One is tempted to ask: Is Paton by this token trying to ide-
alise the African before his white comrades; is he trying to
make him a symbol of "tenderness frustrated" yet not giving
a mere murmur but agreeing to wither with time? Does he
want to portray people like Rev. Kumalo as the sacrificial
lamb that only expresses his pain by a faint tremor of the
body? Or, is Paton trying to tell the white oppressors—'be-
hold a man who suffers immensely without complaining, do
you not admire his long-suffering?'

If this is what interests Paton one would be forced to ask:
'and so what?' Would this parable and sermonising bring a
change of heart in the white oppressors? Would it make
them restore what they have forcibly appropriated to themselves? I think that this journalistic exercise—showing us a
weeping people and asking us to respect and pity them, is
quite inadequate a solution to the reality of the black man's
predicament in racist South Africa. It could, at best, give us
cue for action but it is not positive action in itself.

AFRICAN WRITERS SHOULD BE POLITICALLY COMMITTED

Today, the African writer is not content with only exposing
the sufferings of his people for the world to see. He is now
concerned with how to devise a positive solution to the problems of his people. It is interesting as well as encouraging
that a good number of African writers and critics have and
are still showing concern for the welfare of the masses. They
have convincingly shown that they are on the side of the
people, that they are concerned with how to improve their
living conditions, with how to do everything possible to
make the future bright for them and their children.

In this regard, it was [Chinua] Achebe who shot the first
bullet. He recognises the dual role of the artist in his society:
to give a sense of direction to the people and to identify with
their problems. Achebe thus expresses the need for the
writer to be relevant to his society, to concern himself with
politics when he tells us among other things that

> . . . an African creative writer who tries to avoid the big social
> and political issues of contemporary Africa will end up being
> completely irrelevant—like the absurd man in the proverb who
> leaves his burning house to pursue a rat fleeing from the flames.

In *Cry, The Beloved Country,* Rev. Kumalo is like that "absurd
man" who leaves reality and pursues shadows. He weeps
when he should confront the enemy. He prays when he

should use his position to lead his people in an organised revolt against the oppressive system of his country.

Other than Achebe, there are other African writers and critics who believe that the African writer should concern himself with politics. For example, late Professor Ogungbesan had rightly pointed out that

> The writer is a member of society and his sensibility is conditioned by the social and political happenings around him (because) these issues form part of the substance of life within which his instinct as a writer must struggle.

It is because of this concern that the late Professor had readily recognized Leopold Senghor's wise remark that "African Literature is politically committed". Said Professor Ogungbesan in affirmation:

> It could hardly have been otherwise, for if we cannot now say that colonialism gave rise to Modern African Literature (we can rightly say that) the colonial situation very much 'influenced that literature.'

Similarly, Professor Egudu shares the same view that the writer should be politically committed though this commitment need not demand his becoming a politician or carrying the gun. He writes:

> The essence of commitment in literature consists in the orientation of the writer's mental attitude, his moral constitution, and the expression or manifestation of these can only be implicit (since literature is an art of indirection, of suggesting, not stating) in the writer's verbal structure, mood, tone, and the general rhythmical pattern of his work. Thus socio-political commitment in literary works does not mean actual participation if he is to justify his claim to that position of social regulator and barometer of social morality which is associated with him.

But, other than serving as the barometer for measuring and regulating the mores and values of his society, the writer should not sit on the fence. He should either be on the side of revolt or he is against it. He should be actively involved through the medium of his pen in the struggle to improve the living conditions of the masses in his society.

PATON'S CHARACTERS, FLAT

This is what Alan Paton fails to do in his *Cry*. Although he could have been influenced by and deeply concerned about the predicament of blacks in South Africa (and this he amply shows in this novel) he seems to be more concerned with the Liberal philosophy of brotherly love. He does not give a sense of direction to both the oppressors and the oppressed, nor does he provide us with a character who is determined to fight against the oppressive rule of the whites. It is largely because of the noncommitment of Paton's characters to fight against a system that oppresses them that Ezekiel Mphahlele sees them as 'flat'. Says Mphahlele:

> Paton's characters are nearly all flat. We can almost hear them groan under the load of the author's monumental sermon, a sermon packed with a very deep sincerity (though without deep commitment), the text of which is 'comfort in Desolation'.

But this sermon is not realistic since it would not stop oppression in racist South Africa. The author believes like his chief character, Rev. Kumalo, that love is the solution to the problems of the oppressed blacks. It is doubtful how love would work, when fear rules the lives of both races in South Africa. Rev. Kumalo notices this deadly fear, but the narrator, in spite of this, still tenaciously clings to his love theory which he strongly believes would conquer this fear:

> And now for all the people of Africa, the beloved country (Rev. Kumalo ponders) Nkosi Sikelel': Afrika, God save Africa. But he would not see that salvation. It lay afar off, because men were afraid of it. Because, to tell the truth they were afraid of him (the white man), and his wife, and Msimangu, and the young demonstrator. And what was there evil in their desires, in their hunger? That men should walk upright in the land where they were born, and be free to use the fruits of the earth, what was there evil in it? Yet men were afraid, with a fear that was deep, deep in the heart, a fear so deep that they hid their kindness (he means the whites), or brought it out with fierceness and anger, and hid it behind fierce and frowning eyes. They were afraid because they were so few. And such fear could not be cast out, but by love.

Although there is fear among all the races, however, it is the blacks who fear the whites more. The reason is obvious: they have the instrument of destruction at their command. Rev. Kumalo is one of the blacks who terribly fear the white man. Paton believes that salvation for these oppressed blacks who live in fear shall come through love which he expects the whites to give to the former. But Paton fails to realise that today, the aliens still hate and brutalise the blacks, and Rev. Kumalo in his naivety shares the author's belief. Just like Ngotho in *Weep Not, Child* who vaingloriously lays all his hope for the restoration of the lost Kikuyuland on the fulfilment of an ancient Kikuyu prophecy which says that one day, God shall raise a son from the tribe, a son who shall save the tribe from colonial bondage, so does Rev. Kumalo build all his hope on the love that will come from the white oppressors. But unlike Ngotho, Kumalo does not grow. While the erstwhile relatively obtuse Ngotho, who after doses of rebukes from his son, Boro, for being afraid to confront the white man, later comes to realise the need to be involved in the struggle to chase the white man out of Kikuyuland, Rev. Kumalo, who has witnessed the sufferings of his people both in the city and in the shanties, does nothing. Rev. Kumalo's reaction to the death sentence passed on his son is lamentation. While Ngotho takes active part in the strike against the oppressive rulers in his country, while he later chooses to die so that his son's life (Kamau) might be spared and, while breathing his last he could still charge his militant sons to "fight well", Kumalo, on the other hand, is afraid to confront the white enemy. He asks for forgiveness and sympathy from a people, deaf to the cries of their victims.

. . . Although the language flows smoothly like beautiful poetry, in Paton's story things are not smooth for the black characters looming large everywhere. Both in the big cities and in the shanties the people are suffering terribly. Rev. Kumalo is aware of this. He knows that there is a big crack in the erstwhile ordered and peaceful society:

> He told them too of the sickness of the land, and how the grass had disappeared, and of the *dongas* that ran from hill to valley, and valley to hill; how it was a land of old men and women, and mothers and children; and how the maize grew barely to the height of a man; how the tribe was broken, and the house broken, and the man broken; how they went away, many never came back, many never wrote any more. How this was true not only in Ndotsheni, but also in the Lufafa, and the Inhlavini, and the Umkomaas, and the Umzimkulu.

The white man is the cause of this wreckage. He has appropriated to himself the rich and arable land belonging to the blacks. As Paton tells us, the whites and the blacks live in different worlds within the same society. The aliens have conquered the people and their land. They now occupy the place where:

> The grass is rich and matted, you cannot see the soil. It holds the rain and the mist, and they seep into the ground, feeding the streams in every Kloof. It is well-tended, and not too many cattle feed upon it; not too many fires burn it, laying bare the soils. . . .

The aliens have occupied this land and sequel to this have pushed the rightful owners to the poorer areas where:

> The great red hills stand desolate, and the lightning flashes over them, the clouds pour down upon them, the dead streams come to life, full of the red blood of the earth (a symbol of the bleeding black folk). Down in the valleys women scratch the soil that is left, and the maize hardly reaches the height of a man. They are valleys of old men and women, of mothers and children. The men are away, the youngmen and the girls are away. The soil cannot keep them any more.

Since the poor and sterile soil "cannot keep them any more" the black youths are forced to go to the big city to earn their daily bread. For people like John Kumalo, politics means how to get one's daily bread; there is no going back from the city. It is needless to say that Johanesburg, a sprawling city with many skyscrapers, was built on the gold economy mined in the city and in the suburbs. Whereas it is the blacks who provide the cheap labour for the mines sadly enough they get nothing out of the proceeds from the mines. Their pay is not commensurate with their toil. It is the mines which built the gigantic buildings now inhabited exclusively by whites; the mines also built the hospitals, the best and the biggest in tropical Africa yet, they are reserved for whites only. The people live in decay and disease, there is no protection of any kind for them and their children. They are dying in instalments in the big city, in the daily business of trying to live. Yet, there is none among the white authorities who remembers to preach Paton's sermon of brotherly love, not even the white priests.

THE CRIME WAVE

Like the David-Absalom story in the Bible, Paton's story stresses love, rebellion and forgiveness. In the Bible, Absalom rebels against his father to the extent of raising an army against the King. In the circumstance, the youth is killed. The King, despite Absalom's rebellion, is willing to forgive his transgressing son if ever he survives the war. His primary concern is to hear that the youth is safe. He seems to be so selfish about the safety of his son that he forgets to think of other victims of this war caused by his son. To him these victims on either side are not worth half a ducat.

Similarly, Rev. Kumalo seems to be only concerned about his son who has rebelled against an oppressive system that has now condemned him to death without showing mercy, love and forgiveness which we have just noticed in King David. I think that Paton should not have been only attracted by the story of David and Absalom in the Bible without putting the link succinctly, without stressing the moral message therein—sin, forgiveness and love which very much attracts him. He should have redeemed his white compatriots by forcing it on them to show mercy and love as David did. He should not have allowed his chief character to weep and plead in vain to a people who are not ready to show either mercy or love, a people who are ready to see Absalom executed. Rev. Kumalo does not remember to ask what has caused the strange transformation in Absalom, the son of a priest. He hears that there is a continuous wave of crime among the youths in the city but he fails to ask why these black youths have decided to confront their white enemies through this method. In spite of his bitter experiences in the city and in the shanty towns, in spite of the revelation made to him by his friend, Msimangu, Kumalo would not think of how to fight for his oppressed people. Msimangu shows him the true picture of life in the society:

> My friend, I am a Christian. It is not in my heart to hate a white man. It was a white man who brought my father out of darkness. But you will pardon me if I talk frankly to you. The tragedy is not that things are broken. The tragedy is that they are not mended again. But the house that is broken, the man that falls apart when the house is broken, these are the tragic things. That is why children break the law, and the old white people are robbed and beaten.

An intelligent understanding of the problem indeed! There is one thing which is very clear about the wave of crime in the city. It is the oppressed's reaction to an oppressive system. If anything, it reveals the people's feelings; it shows that they are not happy with the status quo. It is needless saying that as long as the blacks are denied their basic human rights by these aliens, this wave of crime will always be on the increase.

THE IRONY OF ARTHUR'S DEATH

It is however ironical and unfortunate too that the man with a vision, the man who is committed to the problems of the black man, the man with the right ideas and the man who knows the answer, dies prematurely before his ideas could take root. That man is Arthur Jarvis, the hope of the masses. Before he is brutally killed by Absalom who shoots him out of fear and in self defence, Arthur Jarvis was concluding a treatise entitled: "The Truth About Native Crime", a paper he had intended to present to the oppressive rulers in racist South Africa. It is necessary here to examine the conclusions he arrived at in this essay:

> The truth is that our Christian civilization is riddled through and through with dilemma. We believe in the brotherhood of man, but we don't want it in South Africa. We believe that God endows men with diverse gifts, and that human life depends for its fullness on their employment and enjoyment, but we are afraid to explore this belief too deeply. We believe in help for the underdog, but we want him to stay under. And we are therefore compelled, in order to preserve our belief that we are Christian, to ascribe to Almighty God, Creator of Heaven and Earth, our own intentions, and to say that He created white and black. He gives Divine Approval to any human action that is designed to keep black men from advancement. We go so far as to credit Almighty God with having created black men to hew wood and draw water for white men. We go so far as to assume that He blesses any action that is destined to prevent black men from the full employment of the gifts He gave them. Alongside of these very arguments we use other total inconsistent, so that the accusation of repression may be refuted. We say we withhold education because the black child has not the intelligence to profit by it; we withhold opportunity to develop gifts because black people have no gifts; we justify our action by it; we withhold opportunity to develop gifts because black people have no gifts; we justify our action by it; saying that it took us thousands of years to achieve our own advancement, and it would be foolish to suppose that it will take the black man any lesser time, and that therefore there is no need for hurry. . . .

Will all these ill-conceived intentions and conclusions perceived by the alien administrators about the black man be wiped away by the type of love which Paton advocates for both races? No. It is people like Arthur Jarvis who can bring about the desired change of heart in the white oppressors. Arthur Jarvis knows what is permissible and not in the governance of a people. He knows that governance is a question of give and take. He knows what the individual deserves. His appeal is that the Black South African be given his rightful place in the land of his birth. He is disgusted with the oppressive rule of the alien administrator although he is white. This disgust he shows through the medium of his pen. He argues that before:

> It was permissible to leave native education to those who wanted to develop it. It was permissible to doubt its benefits. But is no longer permissible in the light of what we know. Partly because it made possible industrial development, and

partly because it happened in spite of us, there is now a large urbanized native population. Now society has always, for reasons of self-interest if for no other, educated its children so that they grow up law-abiding, with socialized aims and purposes. There is no other way that it can be done. Yet we continue to leave the education of our native urban society to those few Europeans who feel strongly, about it, and to deny opportunities and money for its expansion. That is not permissible. For reasons of self-interest alone it is dangerous. It was permissible to allow the destruction of a tribal system that impeded the growth of the country. It was permissible to believe that its destruction was inevitable. But it is not permissible to watch its destruction, and to replace it by nothing, or by so little, that a whole people deteriorates, physically and morally. . . .

ARTHUR JARVIS ROUSES BLACK YOUTH

Arthur Jarvis is now ready to identify with the masses. He is rousing Black Youths from slumber, he is now asking them to demand their rights. These youths have already formed a club—'Claremont African Boys' Club.' By writing to Arthur through their Secretary they have shown appreciation for his identification with the problems of their people. It is hoped that in the near future they would forge into an organised revolt against their exploiters. Perhaps through them we hope to see a militant wing of dedicated youths like the Mau Mau Freedom fighters in Kikuyuland. One might be tempted to hazard a guess that they could have been the pioneers of the present armed struggle against racism in Zimbabwe, Namibia and in fact, in the whole of racist South Africa.

It is the need to organise the black fold into a fighting force to free themselves from the shackles of racism and colonial bondage that should have been Paton's primary concern and not the love and emotion which he concerns himself with. It is partly because of his posture of non-violence in the struggle to restore the oppressed Black South African to his ancestral heritage that compels Dennis Brutus while summarising Paton's story to frown at his sermon:

> If you know *Cry, The Beloved Country*, you will know that it
> is a rather simple story. It is a narration of a black man's con-
> tact with a society which he doesn't really understand—a so-
> ciety in which he finds himself sucked into the elements of
> that society. He ends as a criminal and the society is accused
> of having made him a criminal. All this is really very straight-
> forward and, in a sense, almost trite—and don't think Paton
> himself would mind if one described it in such term.

Brutus goes further to say:

> One must not think in colour categories, but it is very difficult to resist thinking of Alan Paton as a white man, a sympathising white man, a sympathising white man standing outside the South African society with all its complexities and dynamic tensions and reducing it to what is almost a parable, a simple little tale told with a certain lyricism which I think is sometimes false because it is almost like a kind of poetic prose; but telling a story which moved people, and caught people's attention.

As Dennis Brutus rightly observes what Paton's *Cry*, does is to compel our sympathy for and focus our attention on the victims of racism in South Africa. We are invited to weep and not to wield our weapons of attack in order to confront the enemy. Brutus, it seems, does not believe in Paton's political stance of non-violence which implies non-commitment in the predicament of the Black South African. His concluding lines in his evaluation of Paton's *Cry* validate this observation:

> I don't think that Paton's best attack was in *Cry, The Beloved Country*. I think we should read a little pamphlet which he wrote when people were being moved out of their homes, a thing which he calls "The People Wept", which is movingly beautiful, a most poignant document far surpassing *Cry, the Beloved Country*. It may be that Paton's forte is really pamphleteering rather than writing novels.

Cry, the Beloved Country Is Still Relevant After 50 Years

Andrew Foley

In this selection Andrew Foley reconsiders Cry, the Beloved Country and defends the novel from its critics. Foley argues that Paton's novel is as relevant in 1998 as it was in 1948. Andrew Foley is a widely published author and a Senior Lecturer in the Department of English at Johannesburg College of Education. Foley has written on African literature and politics, and has an active interest in Irish literature and in South African sociolinguistics.

As 1998 marks the fiftieth anniversary of the publication of Alan Paton's *Cry, the Beloved Country*, it seems appropriate to offer a reassessment of the value and significance of the novel. . . . A vital part of its meaning [is] its depiction and analysis of South African social and political conditions on the eve of the advent of apartheid. . . . *Cry, the Beloved Country*, far from being inaccurate or reductive in its social analysis, in fact provides a keen insight into the problems facing South African society at the time, an informed and subtle understanding of contemporaneous socio-political debates, and a sensitive appraisal of the possibilities for the country's restoration on a number of different levels.

. . . A key element in the novel's achievement lies in its moving and evocative presentation of the struggle of the two main protagonists, Stephen Kumalo and James Jarvis, towards mutual understanding and reconciliation in the twilight of their years. . . .

In evaluating the quality of Paton's thought as a social

Excerpted from Andrew Foley, "Considered as a Social Record: A Reassessment of *Cry, the Beloved Country*," *English in Africa*, vol. 25, no. 2, October 1998. Reprinted with permission from Rhodes University, South Africa.

commentator, it is important to note that he was not always a proponent of liberal values. He was not born into a liberal-minded family, nor did he display particularly liberal attitudes in the early part of his life. Although he was clearly a decent, moral young man, concerned about his neighbour, and eager to serve his community, he could not be termed a liberal because he had not yet comprehended the importance of what he later identified as the defining characteristic of liberalism in South Africa, "its particular concern with racial justice.". . .

The seminal event which served to precipitate the start of Paton's "learning" about South Africa was his decision at the age of thirty-two—following a life-threatening bout of enteric fever—to take up the post of Principal at Diepkloof Reformatory for African Boys. Speaking of himself in the third person . . . , he comments:

> It opened his eyes. For the first time in his life . . . he saw South Africa as it was. . . . During those years at Diepkloof Reformatory he began to understand the kind of world in which Black people had to live and struggle and die. I won't say that he overcame all racial fear, but I will say that he overcame all racial hatred and prejudice.

Two further crucial events in Paton's life brought him to full liberal consciousness. Firstly, he served on the Anglican Diocesan Commission of 1941 under the chairmanship of Geoffrey Clayton, then Bishop of Johannesburg. . . . As he trenchantly remarks in *Towards the Mountain*, "the bishop's commission . . . didn't change the heart of the nation but it changed me." Secondly, . . . while Paton had been impressed with [Edith Rheinallt-Jones's] work at the South African Institute of Race Relations . . . as well as with her relationships with blacks, whom she treated as absolute equals, his real revelation came at her funeral in 1944 at St George's Presbyterian Church in Johannesburg: scores of people of every colour and creed "had come to honour her memory—their hates and their fears, their prides and their prejudices, all for the moment forgotten." For Paton the experience was profoundly significant:

> In that church one was able to see, beyond any possibility of doubt, that what this woman had striven for was the highest and best kind of thing to strive for in a country like South Africa. I knew then I would never again be able to think in terms of race and nationality. I was no longer a white person

but a member of the human race. I came to this, as a result of many experiences, but this one . . . was the deepest of them all.

. . . Thus, in writing *Cry, the Beloved Country* in 1946, Paton came to the task not as an uninformed neophyte but as a middle-aged professional man with a mature apprehension of racial and political issues in South Africa.

DEPICTION OF SOCIAL PROBLEMS IS ACCURATE

. . . Paton observes that his book is a work of fiction rather than fact in its primary aspects, but he goes on to stress that in terms of its social analysis of South Africa it is both valid and accurate: "In these aspects therefore the story is not true, but considered as a social record it is the plain and simple truth."

Such a claim is of course rhetorically exaggerated, but Paton's basic point is that the novel's depiction of South Africa's social problems. . . is based upon the actual conditions obtaining in the country at that time. Paton's experiences, over ten years, as Principal of Diepkloof Reformatory had placed him personally and directly in touch with the effects of racial discrimination in South Africa, at the level both of the individual and of the society at large. Furthermore, as a social analyst and commentator, he had over a long period of time wrestled with the question of the underlying causes of these effects, and had frequently presented statistical and other evidence before various public and private bodies. . . .

Clearly, then, the details of the "social record" which emerge in *Cry, the Beloved Country* derive not from unsubstantiated imaginative fancy but from direct personal experience and authentic knowledge of social conditions. It is these details with which Paton confronts the reader in the first movement of the novel, through his presentation of the parallel experiences of Stephen Kumalo and James Jarvis as they are forced to recognise and to understand the nature and the full extent of their society's problems for the first time in their lives.

. . . Kumalo, a humble village parson in Ndotsheni in rural Natal, is compelled into a journey to Johannesburg to try to find three missing members of his family and re-unite the family structure. The attempt ends in failure. . . . Stephen's quest does, nevertheless, serve an important purpose in that it forces him into a greater understanding of himself and his society. He has simply never been fully confronted by the fundamental problems of his society at large and has no experience of how to deal with them. He now embarks not merely on a physical journey but also on a spiritual journey of discovery and learning. . . .

In Johannesburg, then, Kumalo is brought face to face with the poverty and squalor of the townships; he is appalled by the descent into crime, wrongdoing and corruption of so many people, including his own relatives; he is confronted everywhere in the city by the fact of white oppression, racial inequality and injustice; and he is horrified by the infrastructural inadequacies of African life in the city as a whole. . . .

What Kumalo comes fundamentally to understand is that the root cause of this degradation and corruption lies in the disintegration of traditional African society. . . . However, even in this moment of dark despair, there is already forming in his mind an incipient thought about the possibility of a way forward in restoration:

> He turned with relief to the thought of rebuilding. . . . After seeing Johannesburg he would return with a deeper understanding to Ndotsheni. . . . One could go back knowing better the kind of thing that one must build. He would go back with a new and quickened interest in the school, not as a place where children learned to read and write and count only, but as a place where they must be prepared for life in any place to which they might go. Oh for education for his people, for schools up and down the land, where something might be built that would serve them when they went away to the towns, something that would take the place of the tribal law and custom. . . .

Thus, already present at this point in the novel—barely a third of the way through—is the implicit faith in the potential for the regeneration of society. Indeed, it is part of the general ethos of the book that even though the world might seem to be pervaded by evil and destruction there still remain many sources of goodness and generosity, and so it is possible for there to be, at least potentially, in the words of the novel's sub-title, "comfort in desolation.". . . It also suggests that there is enough humaneness and practical goodwill in the world for the beloved country to be regenerated as a just and racially harmonious society. For example, although Kumalo is confronted continually by the injustice of a political system of white oppression, so too does he meet several instances of white men who have dedicated themselves to fighting that system and aiding the oppressed: the

Afrikaner official at the Reformatory; Father Vincent at the mission; Mr Carmichael, the lawyer who takes Absalom's case pro deo; the white motorists who help the bus boycotters; and, of course, Arthur Jarvis himself.

It is, in fact, clearly part of the novel's main purpose to make plain that the large proportion of blame for the current disintegration of black society in South Africa is to be laid squarely at the door of the whites, and so it is in large measure their responsibility to make amends and help to construct a new, integrated and equitable social order. . . .

Msimangu raises two vital issues in the novel: the responsibility of whites to participate actively in the restoration of society; and the pervasive fear which militates against their doing so. If the chorus of African voices in chapter 9 serves to confirm the extensiveness of the frustration and hardship suffered by black South Africans, then the corresponding chorus of white voices in chapter 12 emphasises the ubiquitous fear and confusion in white society generally:

> Have no doubt it is fear in the land. For what can men do when so many have grown lawless? Who can enjoy the lovely land, who can enjoy the seventy years, and the sun that pours down on the earth, when there is fear in the heart? . . . There are voices crying what must be done, a hundred, a thousand voices. But what do they help if one seeks for counsel, for one cries this, and one cries that, and another cries something that is neither this nor that.

ONE WHITE MAN'S CHANGE

Paton's response is to provide a portrait of one white man who does manage to move beyond his own prejudices and fears towards a greater understanding not only of the fundamental problems of his country, but also of the urgent necessity of attempting to solve them.

Like Stephen Kumalo, James Jarvis is a basically decent man living a sedentary farmer's life in the Natal hills. His quiet, comfortable world is shattered, however, by the news of his son's murder in his home in Parkwold, Johannesburg. As a result, he is led, again like Kumalo, on a quest to Johannesburg for his son, which becomes a voyage of discovery and learning about himself and his society. Although his son is already dead when he begins his journey, his search is to understand his son, through his writings and achievements, as he had never done when he was alive.

Jarvis readily admits that "my son and I didn't see eye to

eye on the native question," but he is led into a re-appraisal of his son's views and devotion to the cause of racial justice partly as a result of his son's writings which he encounters in Johannesburg and partly because of his realisation of the extent of his son's reputation and accomplishments. His son's brother-in-law and friend, John Harrison, pays tribute to his standing in the community, and this is confirmed by the extensive media coverage and the many and diverse sympathy notes which follow his death, but most especially by the numerous guests of all creeds and colours who attend his funeral. As a result . . . Jarvis undergoes his own spiritual and political enlightenment and comes to question and eventually reject his previously held conventional and conservative views. . . .

Significantly, before Jarvis leaves to return to Natal, two incidents occur which reveal how his attitudes have changed. In the first, he coincidentally encounters Stephen Kumalo himself at Springs, where he had gone with his wife to visit her niece, Barbara Smith. Kumalo in turn is there to look for

---

THE STORIES OF APARTHEID VICTIMS

Susan Gallagher describes how public airing of apartheid victims' stories contributes to creating a new national identity for South Africa.

These hearings [of the Truth and Reconciliation Commission] are highly structured in a liturgical fashion. Each hearing is opened with a prayer—sometimes Christian, sometimes Muslim, sometimes Jewish—and a large, white candle representing truth is solemnly lit. The audience is then asked to rise out of respect for the victims and their families when they file in. In typical court settings, spectators would rise when the judge comes in; here we rose for the victims. The seven commissioners in attendance then came down from their white linen–clad tables to welcome the victims—by shaking hands, embracing, kissing. Many of the victims were already sobbing, overcome by the mere fact that an official government representative was showing them respect.

As each victim, often accompanied by two or three family members, went up to testify, a psychotherapist sat by his or her side. Before the testimony began, one commissioner asked about the victim's family—parents, spouse, children, siblings—their names, ages, where they lived, how they were employed. This was more than a strategic ploy to put the vic-

Sibeko's daughter as he has promised to do. Kumalo, in great distress, reveals to Jarvis that it was his own son who murdered Jarvis's son. Despite his shock, Jarvis treats the old man with kindness, unlike Smith's daughter, and the mutual respect shown by the two bereaved men foreshadows their closer contact later on. In the second incident, Jarvis gives John Harrison an envelope containing one thousand pounds for the Claremont African Boys' Club. . . .

In addressing the question of the nature and form of the solutions which are advanced in *Cry, the Beloved Country,* it is useful to begin by considering some of the various criticisms levelled against this aspect of the novel. Most of the criticism directed against *Cry, the Beloved Country* is of two kinds: in the first place, the novel is accused of embodying a paternalistic attitude towards Africans; in the second, it is condemned for its political naïveté and the ideological inadequacy of its vision for the practical transformation of South African society.

The tone for the first form of criticism—that of paternalism—is set by an anonymous writer for the *Times Literary*

tim at ease; rather this ritual grounded or located the victim as a person in the fullest African sense—with a family, a community, a place. . . .

The Truth and Reconciliation Human Rights hearings are an unusual instance in which the "hard-to-see" have been made visible. Apartheid South Africa was deliberately structured in numerous legal, social, cultural, and economic ways to silence those who were demonized as "other." The TRC process, in response, was designed to restore "the human and civil dignity" of the victims of apartheid by giving them a collective opportunity to tell their stories, to fashion new public narratives and identities.

Given the significant role that the Christian church played in both the creation of and struggle against apartheid, it is fitting that this attempt to exorcise the past draw on the Christian tradition. South African theologian John De Gruchy says, "The Christian understanding of repentance, forgiveness, and reparation is of fundamental importance in shaping a national consciousness that can heal the land, achieve genuine reconciliation, and build a moral and democratic culture." In this public, communal act of confession, South Africa is beginning to create a new national identity.

Susan Gallagher, *Christianity Today,* February 8, 1998

Supplement [who] assert[s] that, because the political situation has changed so much since *Cry, the Beloved Country* was published in 1948, the novel has come to be "regarded by many who would have praised it then as an old-fashioned, paternalistic book, which portrays Africans in a sentimental and unrealistic light." This line of attack is picked up by Ezekiel Mphahlele in *The African Image* (1962) and developed in some detail by Paul Rich (1985), who argues that the novel is in essence a nostalgic pastoral romance with little sense of historical reality, and he claims that

> the novel completely bypasses the emerging black culture of the townships and slums of the Witwatersrand, which are seen only through the deadening lens of Paton's paternalistic moralism that had been fortified by his experiences as Warden of the Diepkloof Reformatory for "delinquent" African boys outside Johannesburg.

The give-away phrase in this quotation is "delinquent," placed in emphatic inverted commas in an attempt to imply that Paton himself patronisingly regarded his charges as "delinquents." Such an attempt reveals that Rich is either alarmingly unfamiliar with Paton's attitudes and work at Diepkloof (Paton deliberately replaced the title "Warden" with "Principal," and strove to transform the institution from a corrective to an educative one) or he is deliberately distorting the facts to bolster his critique. Similar strictures could be levelled against the *Times Literary Supplement* writer, who seems quite mistaken in stating that Paton knew little of the "African struggle" before writing *Cry, the Beloved Country* and only became familiar with South African politics much later; as well as against Mphahlele, who makes several disturbingly inaccurate assertions such as that Stephen Kumalo in the novel "remains the same suffering, child-like character from beginning to end" when the novel is clearly concerned with his maturation and development. . . .

The second line of criticism has centred around the view that Paton's liberal outlook is jejune [childish] and inefficacious [ineffective] in dealing practically with South Africa's real social problems. Once more, a good deal of such criticism often seems unjust and inaccurate. . . .

Stephen Watson (1982) maintains that Paton in *Cry, the Beloved Country*

> advances the solution of love. . . . Of course, this is useless; the problem has not been caused by a lack of love in South Africa

and therefore to prescribe an antidote of love for it is simply naïve and beside the point.

. . . Watson's assertion that Paton's proposals for social transformation may be reduced to a plea for increased personal love reveals that Watson has failed to comprehend what the term "love" means in the context of the novel. . . .

In what has often been misrepresented by antagonistic critics as a series of empty paternalistic gestures, Jarvis provides help in the form of resources at a basic material level. As has already been noted, he donates one thousand pounds to the Claremont Boys Club, a huge sum of money in those days. . . . Back in Natal, he provides milk to the black schoolchildren of Ndotsheni when he learns of their shortage from his grandson. And he supplies the materials to repair Kumalo's leaky church, whose dilapidation he notices during his visit there. It is important to see that these actions are not designed as terminal solutions, but as short-term measures to meet urgent needs. Jarvis does not perform them in a patronising manner, or out of a desire to establish himself in a position of control over the people, or out of some misplaced sense of guilt. On the contrary, he acts from a wish to lend real practical assistance where it is manifestly necessary; in the spirit, one might say, of Archbishop Clayton, who was wont to suggest that, in times of difficulty about what to do, one should "do the next right thing." As such, Jarvis's actions, coming from a man who had hitherto not even noticed the needs of the people around him, let alone addressed them, represents real moral progress.

. . . At a second level, [Jarvis] seeks to facilitate a more permanent and extensive upliftment of the people of Ndotsheni through the restoration of the land, which has become waste through poor farming methods as well as the drought. To help achieve this, he hires a young black agricultural demonstrator, Napoleon Letsisi, whose task it is to teach the people more modern and successful farming techniques, and thus to help them to help themselves. Jarvis's intention, therefore, is to empower the people to become agriculturally and financially autonomous and self-supporting rather than in any way dependent upon either his skills or his largesse. Once more, it is difficult to see in this case how charges of paternalism may be made against this aspect of the novel. . . .

For Kumalo's part, he too . . . seeks actively to effect some positive changes:

> Kumalo began to pray regularly in his church for the restoration of Ndotsheni. But he knew that was not enough. Somewhere down here upon the earth men must come together, think something, do something.

However, his initiative proves at first a failure: his visits to the chief and the headmaster bear no fruit, because the chief is a mere figurehead with no insight and no real power, and the headmaster, though well-intentioned, is hopelessly out of touch with the everyday needs of the people. . . . Nevertheless, despite Kumalo's failure to mobilise the leaders of the community into effective action, the novel suggests that through his and Jarvis's combined actions—a white man and a black man coming together and thinking and acting in concert—the land may at least partly be restored, an idea symbolically emphasised by the fact that the drought breaks when they commune together in Kumalo's church. . . .

THE NOVEL'S SPIRITUAL THEME

The third level at which the possibility of restoration is explored is the spiritual. Paton remained a deeply committed Christian all his life, and his vision in this novel of the restoration of the land and its people is suffused by his Christian belief in a God who is not merely transcendent but coterminously immanent in the world and involved in human life. . . .

Paton insisted on the crucial affinity between his liberal political ideals and his Christian beliefs. He has stated, for instance, that: "Because I am a Christian I am a passionate believer in human freedom, and therefore, in human rights." . . .

> Now although the Liberal Party is not a Christian organisation, its policies have a great deal in common with Christian ethics. . . . If one is a Christian, one believes that there is a spiritual order as well as a temporal, but one also believes that the values of the spiritual order—*justice, love, mercy, truth* [italics added]—should be the supreme values of the temporal society,—and that the good state will uphold and cherish them. . . .

This is not to suggest, of course, that Christianity and liberalism are interchangeable or identical, but simply that for Paton certain cardinal values are shared by both. . . .

A fourth level at which the text offers a sense of the possibility of restoration [is], namely, the political. This specifically political aspect is conveyed through both the words and the deeds of the various characters in the book. Most obviously, something very close to the liberal political views of Paton himself and other leading liberals of the day is expressed through the writings of Arthur Jarvis. . . . The views expressed in these pieces are lent an urgent immediacy of context through the character, Msimangu, who acts as Kumalo's intellectual as well as physical guide in Johannesburg. It is he, as has been noted, who asserts that the tribe is broken beyond mending and who insists on the moral responsibility of whites to aid in the development of a new society. It is he also who speaks of the practicalities involved in a transition to a new society where political power will be shared between black and white. Just as Msimangu is scrupulously honest in holding whites largely culpable for the present social and political problems in the country, so he is candid in warning of the dangers inherent in a sudden acquisition of power by the oppressed. Such power, he feels, may very likely become "corrupted" through pride or greed or desire for revenge, and so it is crucial that this power be informed by love:

> But there is only one thing that has power completely, and that is love. Because when a man loves he seeks no power, and therefore he has power. I see only one hope for this country, and that is when white men and black men, desiring neither power nor money, but desiring only the good of their country, come together to work for it.

. . . It is this speech of Msimangu's, which is repeated at the end of the novel, that has particularly led to the novel's condemnation by critics like Stephen Watson (1982) for offering a solution based on love rather than hard political theory. Yet it is, in fact, a speech precisely about politics. What it is vital to understand is that by "love" as it is used here, Paton—via Msimangu—does not mean simply some vague notion of interpersonal goodwill. More properly, the term, "love," may be glossed here as the desire to create and live in a just society, and so the act of loving may be thought of as right political conduct which will help bring about a more equitable socio-political order where all persons can live as freely and fully as possible. It ought, in any event, to be clear from the political context of Msimangu's remarks that he visualises such love in terms of black and white South Africans actively and selflessly working together for "the good of their country" as a whole. This understanding of the political meaning of love lies at the centre of the liberal enterprise, which upholds the principle of social and political corrigibility and amelioration [betterment], and believes in the general will and desire of the majority of persons to live under a just system of government. . . .

It is important to see that characters like Arthur Jarvis and Msimangu do take active steps to change their society. Msimangu, as Tony Morphet (1983) points out, "is exemplary in showing what to do," tirelessly striving to improve the welfare of his fellow South Africans and inspiring others, like Stephen Kumalo, to emulate his efforts. Similarly, Arthur Jarvis does not simply write articles and correspond with an African boys club, as Mphahlele suggests, but is actively involved in numerous charitable and social organisations, from Toc H and the YMCA to the Society of Christians and Jews and various African social groups. Moreover, he has . . . intervened directly in the socio-economic sphere, calling for "more Native schools," protesting "about the conditions at the non-European hospital," and insisting on "settled labour" on the mines. In so doing, he shows not only courage and compassion, but also a sound grasp of the social and economic roots of many of his country's problems, as well as an understanding of the basic need for racial equality in the fields of education and health care, and the elimination of unjust labour practices like the migrant worker system. Far from seeming naïve and uninformed, as Stephen Watson avers, Paton, in *Cry, the Beloved Country,* reveals an ability to comprehend and address the fundamental problems of his country in a way which even from this vantage point in time appears remarkably perspicacious and illuminating.

What Paton refuses to condone in this novel . . . is what Watson calls social and political "revolution," to be brought about through the use of violence, if necessary. Throughout his life, Paton resisted any notion of violent revolution, not because he felt personally threatened by it, but because he believed that it would do more harm than good. . . .

LONG-TERM QUESTIONS

In fact, Paton's awareness of the difficulties involved in the regeneration of his society is again underlined when he raises a further thorny problem by linking the literal, agricultural restoration of the land with the political question of land ownership. Paton successfully weaves the issue into the story through the character of the young, politically conscious agricultural demonstrator, Napoleon Letsisi, who is hired by James Jarvis to teach the Ndotsheni community more modern farming methods. In response to Kumalo's praise of Jarvis, Letsisi remarks,

> Umfundisi, it was the white man who gave us so little land, it was the white man who took us away from the land to go to work. And we were ignorant also. It is all these things together that have made this valley desolate. Therefore, what this good white man does is only a repayment.

This deeply problematic question of second-generation rights and the redistribution of the wealth is clearly too much for the old man, however, and, indeed, it is not brought to any definite resolution in the novel. For instance, though James Jarvis is to leave his farm to live in Johannesburg, Paton stops short of suggesting that farmers like Jarvis should relinquish their land, or that they should be encouraged to sell off part of their farms in order to equalise land ownership. This tension between property rights and economic equality remains a problem to this day, however, and Paton could hardly have been expected to resolve it in *Cry, the Beloved Country*. It is to his credit, in fact, that he presents the issue in all its difficulty, and that he refuses to offer any glib or facile proposals for its solution. . . .

This refusal to offer facile utopian solutions to complex problems, represents some of the greatest strengths of liberalism, and may well help to explain the remarkable success of the novel. Far from descending into crude propaganda or arid theorisation, the novel manages to expose and explore some of the central social concerns of South Africa in a way which is moving, honest and enlightening. Moreover, while it remains deeply aware of the intensity and extent of the problems it identifies, it retains a sense of hope, however tentative, for the future, based not upon naïve idealism, but upon a fundamental belief in the power of humankind's innate desire for freedom and justice to prevail.

. . . Throughout the apartheid period, *Cry, the Beloved Country* represented a source of humane political principles and served as a powerfully influential document of social protest in South Africa. Although it is true that several novels up to that time had dealt with what was rather loosely referred to as "the native question"—most notably William Plomer's *Turbott Wolfe* (1925) and Peter Abrahams's *Mine Boy* (1946)—none had done so in as comprehensive, insightful and moving a fashion.

Christopher Hope (1985) has rightly termed *Cry, the Beloved Country* "the great exemplar" of protest novels in South Africa, of "powerful works which lay bare the evil of apartheid." Jack Cope (1970), moreover, has claimed that *Cry, the Beloved Country* ushered in "a new period" in South Africa's literary history and that "with this book, South African fiction really came into its own," not least of all because "there is a new awareness in it of the man on the other side of the barbed wire, a true fellow-feeling between white and black as we had never had before."

Following the demise of apartheid, the popularity and influence of *Cry, the Beloved Country* and Paton's work in general has, if anything, increased. . . . There are several reasons for the continued interest in Paton and especially his first great novel. The most obvious is that *Cry, the Beloved Country* is a fine work of art, in which vital social and political issues emerge organically and coherently from vivid, moving details of plot and characterisation. Another is that many of the problems and debates raised in the novel persist in the South Africa of today as the country struggles to throw off the injustices of the past and to normalise itself. Problems such as unemployment, poverty, insufficient housing, inadequate educational opportunities, as well as, most evidently, the unacceptably high crime rate, remain crucially pertinent. In fact, reading the novel today inspires the uncanny feeling that, in terms of its portrayal of social ills, it might have been written in 1998 rather than 1948.

The one great difference, of course, is that South Africa has managed to transform itself into a constitutional liberal democracy. Had Paton lived, he would no doubt have been deeply gratified that his vision of a just political dispensation had been achieved and that it had come about through peaceful negotiated means. On the other hand, he would also, no doubt, have spoken out against corruption and the seeming inability of the government to deal effectively with many of the social problems identified above. His wise counsel and insight are preserved, however, in his books, especially in *Cry, the Beloved Country.* Above all, the continuing relevance of the novel lies in the principles and values which underpin it: the courage to confront social problems honestly and openly; the resolve to take action to alleviate such problems; and a faith in the power of ordinary individuals to take responsibility for themselves and their communities in improving the quality of life. The example set by Stephen Kumalo and James Jarvis remains no less relevant and important today than it was half a century ago.

Chronology

1903

Alan Stewart Paton born to James and Eunice Paton on January 11 in Pietermaritzburg, the capital of Natal, a province in South Africa.

1907

Brother, Atholl, born.

1908

Enters first grade, already able to read and write.

1914

Enters Maritzburg College in Pietermaritzburg, South Africa, roughly equivalent to an American high school.

1918

Joins Student Christian Association with friend Railton Dent.

1919–22

Attends Natal University College in Pietermaritzburg on scholarship; graduates with a bachelor of science in math and physics.

1923

Sent to London and Cambridge by fellow students to represent them at the Imperial Council of Students.

1924–1935

Teaches school, including Ixopo High School and Maritzburg College.

1926

With two friends founds Students' Christian Association boys' camp in Natal.

1928

Marries Doris (Dorrie) Olive Lusted.

1930

Father dies. First son, David, born.

1931

Joins the Anglican Church.

1933

Gold discovered at Odendaalsrust in the Orange Free State province of South Africa.

1934

Completes with highest honors the examination for a master's degree in education at Natal University College, but never finishes the required thesis. (Granted an honorary degree in 1961.)

1935

Nearly dies from typhoid fever.

1935–48

Serves as Principal at Diepkloof Reformatory outside South Africa's largest city, Johannesburg.

1936

Second son, Jonathan, born. Joins South African Institute of Race Relations.

1938

Goes on the Great Trek, the Afrikaner Centenary celebration. Disillusioned by ultra-Afrikaner nationalism.

1939

Brother Atholl killed in action in World War II. Volunteers for military service; not taken because his reformatory work is deemed vital. Becomes national chairman of YMCA.

1942–43

Writes articles for magazines and newspapers and speaks on crime and punishment.

1946

Begins *Cry, the Beloved Country* in Trondheim, Norway. Completes it while on international tour to study reformatories and prisons.

1947

Aubrey and Marigold Burns, first readers of his novel, help

Paton choose its title and find a publisher.

1948

February 1, novel is published by Scribner's. February 5, Paton receives first rave review. Resigns from Diepkloof to become a fulltime writer. National Party, elected to lead South Africa, institutes apartheid in the nation.

1949

Receives London *Sunday Times* Book Award. Goes to New York for opening of *Lost in the Stars,* a musical play by Maxwell Anderson and Kurt Weill, based on *Cry, the Beloved Country.*

1950

Becomes second layperson ever accorded honor of preaching a sermon in St. Paul's Cathedral, London. Works in London and Johannesburg with Zoltan Korda on screenplay for the film version of *Cry, the Beloved Country.* South Africa's apartheid government passes Group Areas Act removing 75 percent of the population from their homes to all-black settlements on 13 percent of the land.

1952

Helps found South Africa's Liberal Party to oppose the ruling Nationalist Party's apartheid policies. Begins visits to and friendship with Chief Lutuli of the African National Congress Party (ANC).

1953

Publishes second novel, *Too Late the Phalarope.* Works with Dorrie at a tuberculosis sanatorium for black Africans.

1954

Attends World Council of Churches, in Evanston, Illinois, where he is scribe for the section that reports on "The Church Amid Racial and Ethnic Tensions." Invited by *Collier's* magazine, tours the United States with photographer, Dan Weiner, and writes two articles on race relations in America. Becomes the official leader of the Liberal Party in South Africa. Awarded honorary doctor of humanities degree by Yale University.

1955

Publishes *The Land and People of South Africa* in Britain and the United States.

1957

Works to raise funds for legal defense of Chief Lutuli, Nelson Mandela, and others. Begins writing political column, "The Long View," for *Contact.* Bus boycott held in Alexandra, a black section of Johannesburg, in the province of Transvaal.

1958

Writes a play, *David Livingstone,* later retitled *Last Journey.* Publishes *Confirmation for a Young Boy Confirmed.*

1960

Given Freedom Award in New York. Upon his return to Johannesburg, passport confiscated by South African government. Writes words for a musical play, *Mkhumbane.* At Sharpville in the province of the Orange Free State, South Africa, police kill 69 peaceful demonstrators protesting the Pass Laws.

1961

Publishes a collection of short stories titled *Tales from a Troubled Land* in America, and titled *Debbie Go Home* in Britain and South Africa. Receives Free Academy of Hamburg award (in absentia).

1962

Awarded honorary doctorate of letters by Kenyon College, Ohio (in absentia).

1963

Receives Franklin D. Roosevelt award from Midwood High School, New York.

1964

In court pleads for mitigation of sentence of Mandela and others to help avoid death penalty. Mother dies. Publishes *South African Tragedy: The Life and Times of Jan Hofmyer,* for which he receives the annual CNA literary award. Publishes a play, *Sponono,* written with Krishna Shaw and based on one of Paton's short stories.

1966

Security police raid Paton's home.

1967

Dorrie Olive Paton dies of emphysema.

1968

Prohibition of Interference Act banning interracial meetings causes demise of Liberal Party. Publishes *Instrument of Thy Peace*, based on the prayer associated with St. Francis of Assisi. Awarded honorary doctorate of letters from University of Natal.

1969

Publishes *For You Departed* in honor of Dorrie. Marries his secretary, Anne Margaret Hopkins.

1971

Passport restored by South African Government, Paton accepts honorary doctorate of letters from Harvard, honorary doctorate of letters from Trent University in Ontario, and honorary doctor of divinity from Edinburgh University.

1972

Awarded honorary doctorate of letters from Rhodes University in Grahamstown in the province of Cape Town, South Africa.

1973

Publishes *Apartheid and the Archbishop: The Life and Times of Geoffrey Clayton* which receives the annual CNA literary award.

1974

Publishes *Knocking on the Door*, an anthology. Awarded honorary doctor of letters from Willamette University, Salem, Oregon.

1975

Awarded honorary doctor of laws degree from the University of Witwatersrand in Johannesburg. Publishes *Knocking on the Door*.

1976

Meets privately with United States secretary of state Cyrus Vance to promote universal suffrage and majority rule for South Africa. South African police kill 575 people in the Soweto uprising against apartheid.

1977

Awarded honorary doctorate of letters from the University of Michigan.

1980

Publishes *Toward the Mountain*, first volume of autobiography, 1903–1948.

1981

Publishes third novel, *Ah, But Your Land Is Beautiful.*

1982

Tours in the United States with Anne Paton.

1986

Lectures at Harvard and at LaSalle University, Philadelphia. Awarded honorary doctorate of humanities by LaSalle University and honorary doctorate of letters by the University of Durban-Westville, South Africa.

1988

Dies at home April 12. *Journey Continued,* second volume of autobiography, 1948–1988, published posthumously.

FOR FURTHER RESEARCH

ABOUT ALAN PATON

Peter F. Alexander, *Alan Paton: A Biography.* New York: Oxford University Press, 1994.

John D. Batersby, "Author Reflects on Novel of Apartheid and Hope," *New York Times,* April 12, 1988.

Lea Bentel, *Alan Paton: A Bibliography.* Johannesburg: University of the Witwatersrand, Department of Bibliography, Librarianship, and Typography, 1969.

R.M. Brown, "Alan Paton: Warrior and Man of Grace," *Christianity and Crisis,* June 1998.

Herbert Mitang, "Alan Paton, Author and Apartheid Foe, Dies of Cancer at 85," *New York Times,* April 13, 1988.

"Paton, Alan," *Contemporary Literary Criticism.* Farmington Hills, MI: Gale, 1989.

"Paton, Alan," *Current Biography.* New York: H.W. Wilson, May 1988.

Publisher's Weekly, "Three Writers," April 23, 1982.

Humphrey Tyler, "The Cry That Has Echoed for 40 Years: Writer Alan Paton Still Sees Hope for His Beloved Country," *Christian Science Monitor,* March 1, 1988.

CRITICAL WORKS ON ALAN PATON

Sheridan Baker, *Paton's "Cry, the Beloved Country": The Novel, the Critics, the Setting.* New York: Charles Scribner's Sons, 1968.

R.M. Duncan, "The Suffering Servant in Novels by Paton, Bernanos, and Schwarz-Bart," *Christian Scholar's Review,* January 1987.

Edmund Fuller, *Man in Modern Fiction: Some Minority Opinions on Contemporary American Writing.* New York: Random House, 1958.

David Medalie, "'A Corridor Shut at Both Ends': Admonition and Impasse in Van der Post's *In a Province* and Paton's *Cry, the Beloved Country,*" *English in Africa,* vol. 25, no. 2, October 1998.

N. Munger, *Touched by Africa.* Pasadena, CA: Castle Press, 1983.

A. Nash, "The Way to the Beloved Country: History and the Individual in Alan Paton's *Towards the Mountain,*" *English in Africa,* October 1983.

Martin Tucker, *Africa in Modern Literature.* New York: Unger, 1967.

S. Watson, "*Cry, the Beloved Country* and the Failure of Liberal Vision,*" English in Africa,* May 1982.

ABOUT ALAN PATON'S TIME

Laurel Corona, *Modern Nations: South Africa.* San Diego: Lucent Books, 2000.

John M. Dunn, *The Civil Rights Movement.* San Diego: Lucent Books, 1998.

Don Lawson, *South Africa.* New York: Franklin Watts, 1986.

Gary E. McCuen, ed., *The Apartheid Reader,* Hudson, WI: Gary E. McCuen, 1986.

Pictorial History of the 20th Century. North Dighton, MA: J.H. Press, 1995.

WORKS BY ALAN PATON

AUTOBIOGRAPHY

For You Departed. New York: Charles Scribner's Sons, 1969.

Journey Continued, An Autobiography. Charles Scribner's Sons, 1988.

Towards the Mountain. Charles Scribner's Sons, 1980.

BIOGRAPHY

Apartheid and the Archbishop: The Life and Times of Geoffrey Clayton, Archbishop of Cape Town. New York: Charles Scribner's Sons, 1974.

South African Tragedy: The Life and Times of Jan Hofmeyr. New York: Charles Scribner's Sons, 1971.

NOVELS

Ah, But Your Land Is Beautiful. New York: Charles Scribner's Sons, 1982.

Cry, the Beloved Country. New York: Charles Scribner's Sons, 1997.

Too Late the Phalarope. New York: Charles Scribner's Sons, 1995.

PLAYS

Lost in the Stars, with Maxwell Anderson. New York: Sloan

Associates, 1950.

Sponono, with Krishna Shah. New York: Charles Scribner's Sons, 1965. Based on three stories from *Tales from a Troubled Land.*

RELIGIOUS WORKS

"Africa, Christianity, and the West," *Christianity and Crisis,* December 1960.

"The Church Amid Racial Tensions," *Christian Century,* March 1954.

"Church, State and Race," *Christian Century,* February 1958.

Instrument of Thy Peace: Meditations Prompted by the Prayer of St. Francis. New York: Seabury, 1982.

"The Novelist and Christ," with Liston Pope, *Saturday Review,* December 1954.

"The Person in Community," in *The Christian Idea of Education: Papers and Discussion,* ed. Edmund Fuller. New Haven, CT: Yale University Press, 1957.

"Religious Faith and Brotherhood," in *Religious Faith and World Culture,* ed. A.W. Loos. New Haven, CT: Prentice-Hall, 1951.

"Towards a Spiritual Community," *Christian Century,* March 1950.

SHORT STORIES

Tales from a Troubled Land. New York: Charles Scribner's Sons, 1965.

OTHER WRITINGS

"Africa, Awakening, Challenges the World," *New York Times,* July 1952.

"Africa Reporting," *New York Times Book Review,* February 1949.

"Alan Paton Reports on South Africa," *Commonweal,* May 1965.

"America and the Challenge of Africa," *Saturday Review,* May 1953.

"As Blind as Samson Was," *New York Times,* April, 1960.

"The Challenge of Fear," *Saturday Review,* September 1967.

Creative Suffering: The Ripple of Hope. Norman, OK: Pilgrim, 1970.

Go Well, My Child. Washington, D.C.: Smithsonian Institution Press, 1985 (coauthored with Constance Larrabee).

"Grim Drama in Johannesburg," *New York Times,* February 1955.

Hope for South Africa. New York: Praeger, 1959.

"Impending Tragedy," *Life,* May 1953.

"In a World Ruled by Fear," *They Stand Invincible: Men Who Are Reshaping Our World,* ed. R.M Bartlett. New York: Thomas X. Crowell, 1959.

"In Memoriam: Albert Luthuli," *Christianity and Crisis,* September 1967.

Knocking on the Door: Alan Paton/Shorter Writings, ed. Colin Gardner. New York: Charles Scribner's Sons, 1975.

The Land and the People of South Africa. Philadelphia: Lippincott, 1972.

"Liberal Approach," *New York Times,* August 1953.

"A Literary Remembrance," *Time,* April 25, 1988.

The Long View, ed. Edward Callan. New York: Praeger, 1968.

"A Message to the People of South Africa," *Christianity and Crisis,* March 1969.

"Negro in America Today," *Colliers,* October 1954.

"Negro in the North," *Colliers,* October 1954.

"On Trial for Treason," *New Republic,* November 1957.

"A Patriot's Dilemma: Why I Stay in South Africa," *Commonweal,* November 1978.

"A Personal View," *New York Times,* March 1964.

"Republic for Which South Africa Stands," *New York Times,* May 1961.

"The Road," *New Yorker,* December 1960.

Save the Beloved Country, eds. Hans Strydom and David Jones, New York: Charles Scribner's Sons, 1989. Articles written from 1965 to 1987.

"School in Danger," *Christian Century,* December 1955.

South Africa in Transition. New York: Charles Scribner's Sons, 1956.

South Africa Today. New York: Public Affairs Committee, 1951.

"South African Treason Trial," *Atlantic,* January 1960.

"Tragedy of the Beloved Country," *Coronet,* May 1956.

"The Tragic and Lovely Land of South Africa," *Holiday,* February 1957.

"The Unrecognized Power," *Saturday Review,* November 1951.

"White Dilemma in Black Africa," *New York Times,* September 1960.

"The White Man's Dilemma," *Saturday Review,* May 1953.

"The Yoke of Racial Inequality," *New York Times,* November 1968.

INDEX